EGYPTIAN HIEROGLYPHIC GRAMMAR

A Handbook for Beginners

Günther Roeder

DOVER PUBLICATIONS, INC.
Mineola, New York

Bibliographical Note

This Dover edition, first published in 2002, is an unabridged republication of *Short Egyptian Grammar*, published by Humphrey Milford, London, 1920.

Library of Congress Cataloging-in-Publication Data

Roeder, Günther, 1881–1966.
Egyptian hieroglyphic grammar : a handbook for beginners / Günther Roeder.
p. cm.
Originally published: Short Egyptian grammar. London : Humphrey Milford, 1920.
Includes bibliographical references.
ISBN 0-486-42509-6 (pbk.)
1. Egyptian language—Grammar. I. Roeder, Günther, 1881–1966. Short Egyptian grammar. II. Title.

PJ1135 .R5 2002
496'.18421—dc21

2002034978

Manufactured in the United States of America
Dover Publications, Inc., 31 East 2nd Street, Mineola, N.Y. 11501

TO

Mr. JOHN L. MAGEE

THIS ENGLISH EDITION

IS AFFECTIONATELY DEDICATED

BY THE TRANSLATOR

TRANSLATOR'S PREFATORY NOTE.

The ever-growing interest taken in Egyptology has encouraged the hope that an English edition of Dr. Roeder's compact little handbook may prove useful to English-speaking students of the present time. For the beginner in the ancient language of the Egyptians, there is nothing in any language which compares in any way with Dr. Roeder's little book.

As translator, I have followed the original as closely as the English idiom would permit. I have, however, inserted additional references in the bibliographical section, and have here and there tacitly corrected mis-prints and other minor errors. Because of a difference between the English and the German pronunciation of the letter j, I have used y as the transliteration of the Egyptian 𓇋.

It is with great pleasure that I avail myself of the opportunity of expressing my personal thanks to my wife and Miss Walther for assistance in translation, and likewise to the Rev. J. A. Maynard for a number of corrections and helpful suggestions. I wish also to thank the author for his kindness in reading the proof, the printers for the satisfactory accomplishment of their task, and the Yale University Press for their work of publication.

Chicago, July 17th.. 1915.

Samuel A. B. Mercer.

PREFACE OF THE AUTHOR.

When Erman wrote his Egyptian Grammar in 1894, he was confronted with the task of handling for the first time in a scientific manner the hieroglyphics and the Egyptian language. He presented his subject in such a manner, however, that even a beginner could study it. In the later editions, with each of which there is associated an advance in the knowledge and dissemination of more correct conceptions of the Egyptian, Erman's work became broader and deeper, so that it now contains not only the foundations but also practically all the essential details of our grammatical knowledge. Hence, it has naturally become harder for the beginner to understand. Furthermore, since the reading exercises have in part been omitted, the beginner is obliged, even during the first year, to procure in addition to the Grammar a Chrestomathy and a Glossary as well. These cost all together Mk. 43.80.

This state of affairs has induced me to compile this little book for all those who wish to occupy themselves with Egyptian for a few semesters only; or who wish to overcome the first difficulties quickly and begin as soon as possible the reading of the easier texts. Such introductions are found in abundance in other sciences, and have proved of great benefit. It is meant not only to convey the rudiments in a practical manner, in the cheapest possible form, for the benefit of those interested, at the university or in wider circles, but also to place at their disposal for the first year material of the easiest kind, with all the necessary apparatus for reading, writing, and translating. It is hoped that my work will be judged in the light of these circumstances, especially in view of its inexpensiveness.

My presentation of the grammar is based upon Erman's „Grammar", Sethe's „Verbum", and the articles of various authors appearing in the technical journals. In the composition of the individual sections, I have been guided by my own experience in teaching. For the arrangement of other parts of my book, I have had no suitable model. The practical grammars in foreign languages, published in England (Budge, Murray) and in Italy (Farina), have their own peculiarities, to which I am indebted for occasional suggestions. In accordance with the modern method of teaching, employed in all languages, I have considered it my task to bring before the pupil from the very first hieroglyphic examples of the rules. He should thus be able, even after the first lesson, to translate simple sentences independently.

I shall be thankful for any suggested improvements, which are the result of practice; for even the smallest suggestion arising from experience can become of value to the future student. Only do not ask for scientific perfection; that would be impossible under the existing conditions. I am perfectly conscious of the fact that occasionally I have where unavoidable somewhat simplified complicated points of grammar, the double forms of the tense śḏm.f for example, or entirely omitted them. But this book is written for beginners. The omission of references in the reading exercises is intentional, for the beginner does not need to see the complete texts from which the extracts were taken, and the Egyptologist knows them anyway.

Breslau, Christmas 1912.

Günther Roeder.

AUTHOR'S NOTE ON THE ENGLISH EDITION

The state of affairs in connection with English text-books of the Egyptian language is not more satisfactory than that of the German. Professor Breasted's translation of the first edition of Erman's grammar is long since exhausted and outgrown; and Budge's and Murray's introductory books, however useful they may have been, cannot be considered a substitute. Therefore, I have gladly accepted Professor Mercer's kind offer to translate my little Introduction; and students, as well as I, will be thankful for his labour of love.

May Professor Mercer be permitted to see his work crowned with success! America and England have many first rate Egyptian archaeologists, but comparatively few Egyptian philologists; and accordingly the attention of wider circles has been directed more toward excavations and antiquities than toward Egyptian literature. It would be a real delight for German Egyptology, if it could see its philological results made serviceable to the same wider circles, and if thereby the general presentation of the intellectual life of Egypt could be disseminated in a desirable manner.

Hildesheim, Christmas 1915.

Günther Roeder.

The work of printing could not be finished before Christmas 1919. Miss Latona Williams has kindly helped much in reading the proofs and in correcting errors.

CONTENTS.

Literature for Beginners.

Introduction. AD. ERMAN, Die Hieroglyphen, Göschen Series, 1912, 80 Pf., containing a concise sketch of the decipherment and grammar as well as a few texts.

Texts. When the present Grammar and Reading Exercises are finished, the student should attempt texts which are almost or quite complete and which are printed in the form of sentences. Such will be found in AD. ERMAN, Ägyptische Chrestomathie, Berlin, 1904, 12,50 M.; E. A. WALLIS BUDGE, An Egyptian Reading Book, London, 1896, 18 shillings (a series of historical, funeral, moral, religious, and mythological texts printed in hieroglyphic characters together with a transliteration and a complete vocabulary); K. SETHE, Urkunden des Ägyptischen Altertums: IV. Urkunden der 18. Dynastie, 16 Hefte, Leipzig, 1905 ff., each 5 M. The student should not allow the occurrence of occasional words, forms, and constructions which are not clear to hinder his progress, and difficulties will increase when he tackles inscriptions in their original arrangement. For such, see: Staatliche Museen zu Berlin, Ägyptische Inschriften (since 1901, 7 Hefte, Berlin, 1901 ff., each 7,50 M.); Hieroglyphic Texts from Egyptian Stelae, etc., in the British Museum (since 1910, 5 parts, London, 1910 ff., each 7s. 6d.). Then he should copy inscriptions in Museums, Institutes, or Libraries which have originals, plaster casts, or photographs. Then and only then will he learn to understand the peculiarity of the hieroglyphic script and the nature of ancient monuments.

Grammar. AD. ERMAN, Ägyptische Grammatik, 3. Aufl., Berlin, 1911. 18 M. (scientific and complete: first edition translated by James H. Breasted, New York, 1894). K. SETHE, Das ägyptische Verbum, I—II, Leipzig, 1899, 50 M. (fundamental). E. A. WALLIS BUDGE, First Steps in Egyptian, London, 1895, 12 shillings (only a collection of examples for the purpose of learning the use of words, without grammatical treatment). MARGARET A. MURRAY, Elementary Egyptian Grammar, London, 1908, 4 shillings (a brief synopsis of Egyptian grammar without a chrestomathy).

Lexicons. AD. ERMAN, Ägyptisches Glossar, Berlin, 1904, 13 M. (belongs to the Chrestomathie); Zur ägyptischen Wortforschung I—III, Sitzungsberichte der Preussischen Akademie der Wissenschaften, 1907, 1912, Berlin, 3,50 M.; K. SETHE, Verbum III, Indices, Leipzig, 1902, 16 M. (nearly all verbs, but with references to examples). HEINR. BRUGSCH, Hieroglyphisch-demotisches Wörterbuch I—VII, Leipzig, 1867—1882, 820 M. (comprehensive but antiquated).

Coptic. Whoever wishes to understand Egyptian grammar and syntax fully must study Coptic, which furnishes the vowel sounds: G. STEINDORFF, Koptische Grammatik, 2. Aufl., Berlin, 1904, 14 M. M. A. MURRAY, Elementary Coptic (Sahidic) Grammar, London, 1911. Cf. §8d. below.

History. JAMES H. BREASTED, A History of the Ancient Egyptians, New York, 1908, $1.50 (with four maps and three plans; there is a larger edition of the same work with 200 illustrations; $4.80). A. A. WALLIS BUDGE, A History of the Egyptian People, London, 1914 (with illustrations). EDUARD MEYER, Geschichte des Altertums, 2. Aufl., I, 2, Stuttgart-Berlin, 1909, 15 M. (purely scientific with bibliography.)

History of Culture. AD. ERMAN, Life in Ancient Egypt, translated by H. M. Tirard, London and New York, 1894 (with 411 illustrations, comprehensive an fundamental). G. STEINDORFF, Die Blütezeit des Pharaonenreichs, Bielefeld-Leipzig, 1900, 4 M. (with 143 pictures). GÜNTHER ROEDER, Aus dem Leben vornehmer Ägypter, Leipzig, 1912, 1 M. (translations of autobiographies with 16 pictures). HERMANN SCHNEIDER, Kultur und Denken der alten Ägypter, 2. Ausgabe, Leipzig, 1909 (with eight pictures and one map).

Religion. AD. ERMAN, A Handbook of Egyptian Religion, translated from the German by A. S. Griffith, New York, 1907 (with 130 illustrations). GEORG STEINDORFF, The Religion of the Ancient Egyptians, American Lectures on the History of Religions, New York and London, 1905. JAMES H. BREASTED, Development of Religion and Thought in ancient Egypt, New York, 1912, $1.50 (with special reference to the pyramid texts and the Old Testament). GÜNTHER ROEDER, Urkunden zur Religion des alten Ägypten, Jena 1915, 7,50 M. (Translations of texts with introduction and explanations).

Literature. AD. ERMAN und FR. KREBS, Aus den Papyrus der Museen zu Berlin, Berlin, 1899, 4 M. (a collection of translations with 37 specimens of writing). G. MASPERO, Les contes populaires de l'Égypte ancienne, 4. ed., Paris, 1911 (translations of Egyptian literature). E. A. WALLIS BUDGE, The Literature of the Ancient Egyptians, London, 1914, 5 shillings. ALFRED WIEDEMANN, Popular Literature in Ancient Egypt, translated by J. Hutschison, London, 1902. EPIPHANIUS WILSON, Egyptian Literature, Revised Edition, London, and New York, 1901 (comprising Egyptian Tales, Hymns, Litanies, Invocations, the Book of the Dead, and Cuneiform writings). Records of the Past, Egyptian Texts, Vols. IV—VI, London. W. M. F. PETRIE, Egyptian Tales, Vols. I—II, London. 1899.

Art. WILH. SPIEGELBERG, Geschichte der ägyptischen Kunst, Leipzig, 1903, 2 M. (with 79 pictures). F. W. v. BISSING, Einführung in die Geschichte der ägyptischen Kunst, Berlin, 1908, 4 M. (with 32 plates); Denkmäler ägyptischer Skulptur, München, 1906 1911, 240 M. (144 large plates with text). G. MASPERO, Art in Egypt, London, 1912, $ 1.50 (with many pictures). JEAN CAPART, L'Art Égyptien, Série 1—2, Bruxelles, 1909 and 1911, each 10 Fr. (each 100 pictures with short text). W. M. F. PETRIE, Egyptian Decorative Art, London, 1895; Arts and Crafts in Ancient Egypt, London, 1906, 5 shillings.

Museums. Staatliche Museen zu Berlin, Ausführliches Verzeichnis der ägyptischen Altertümer und Gipsabgüsse, 1899, 3 M. (with 83 pictures). G. MASPERO, Guide to the Cairo Museum, 5. ed., Cairo, 1910. LUDWIG BORCHARDT, Works of Art from the Egyptian Museum at Cairo, Cairo, 1908, 25 shillings (50 photographs with short text). E. A. WALLIS BUDGE, A Guide to the Egyptian Collections in the British Museum, London, 1909 (with 53 plates and 180 illustrations in the text). New York, Metropolitan Museum of Art: A Handbook of the Egyptian Rooms, New York, 1911 (with many illustrations). Various reports of accessions to different

Egyptian collections: Bulletin of the Metropolitan Museum of Art, New York; Museum of Fine Arts Bulletin, Boston; Amtliche Berichte aus den Staatlichen Museen, Berlin.

Periodicals. Proceedings of the Society of Biblical Archaeology, London; Zeitschrift für ägyptische Sprache und Altertumskunde, Leipzig; Recueil de travaux relatifs à la philologie et l'archéologie égyptiennes et assyriennes, Paris (all three for the whole field of Egyptology, the last two also for the language). Journal of Egyptian Archaeology, London, Vol. I, 1914; Ancient Egypt, London, Vol. I, 1914 (both especially for excavations). Annales du Service des Antiquités de l'Égypte, Cairo; Orientalistische Literaturzeitung, Leipzig (with bibliography of books and articles). Articles and reports on Egyptology are also to be found in: American Journal of Archaeology, New York; Annals of Archaelogy and Anthropology, Liverpool; Sphinx, Upsala; Jornal of the Manchester Egyptian and Oriental Society, Manchester.

Bibliography. F. Ll. GRIFFITH in Archaeological Report, Egypt Exploration Fund, London, yearly since 1892–1893, and continued in Journal of Egyptian Archaeology. L. SCHERMAN, Orientalische Bibliographie, Vols. I–XXV for 1887–1911. See also the various lists in the periodicals, and the yearly reports in: Jahresberichte der Geschichtswissenschaft, Berlin; Zeitschrift der Deutschen Morgenländischen Gesellschaft, Leipzig; Theologischer Jahresbericht, Leipzig; American Journal of Archaeology, New York.

Chronological Table.

EARLY PERIOD: Predynastic period and Dyn. 1—2. 4000—2000 B. C. § 1.

Primitive culture; beginning of the script.

OLD KINGDOM: Dyn. 3—6 2900—2400 B. C. § 2.

Kings were buried in pyramids (in which are the "Pyramid texts"); rich private persons in Mastabas.

MIDDLE KINGDOM: Dyn. 11—13 2200—1800 B. C. § 3.

Dynasty 12 is the period of classic literature and religion. Secular and religious texts were written on papyrus in hieratic, or engraved and painted in hieroglyphics on the walls of temples and private tombs and coffins.

NEW KINGDOM: Dyn. 17—21 1600—1000 B. C. § 4.

The classic literature of the Middle Kingdom is further continued; gradually more and more elements from the vernacular penetrate into the classic language, and from the hieratic script pass into the hieroglyphics.

LATE PERIOD: (Libyan, Nubian, and Persian supremacy): Dyn. 22—30 1000—332 B. C. § 5.

After the language and orthography had completely degenerated, there was a conscious return to antique words, forms, and writing; the "renaissance" was carried out by the kings of Sais ("Saitic Period").

GRAECO-ROMAN PERIOD: since 332 B. C. § 6.

While in daily life a very slurred vernacular was used—written in the "demotic" script—the priests, studying the religious literature of all past epochs, placed their texts on the walls of the temples in mysterious reinterpreted hieroglyphics which none of the common people could read. The knowledge of the hieroglyphics died out with the last priests of the Egyptian gods, who in remote places served them until the fifth century A. D. The Greek language, which was spoken in Egypt since the last few centuries B. C., entirely replaced the native idiom in the first century A. D.

Nature of the Language and Script.

§ 7. The Egyptian language is related to Semitic languages as well as to the Berber and East African Hamitic languages, and has connections, which are easily traceable, with each individual language of both these groups. The theory of the grafting of a Semitic on to an African language has lately been given up again. If this introduction associates itself closely with the Semitic languages, especially Hebrew, it does so only on superficial grounds: on the one hand, because the history of Semitic languages is better known to us than that of the African; and on the other, because the greater number of those who will use this book will be Semitic and theological students.

§ 8. The most important epochs in the development of the Egyptian language—only one of which is really taken into consideration by this introduction, namely, the classical language—are the following:

a THE ANCIENT LANGUAGE: in the "Pyramid texts" (religious inscriptions of the Old Kingdom). Preserved almost entirely in the hieroglyphics.

b THE CLASSICAL LANGUAGE: in the inscriptions and papyri of the Middle Kingdom; imitated in the official and religious inscriptions of all the following epochs; but became more and more intermingled with vernacular forms and words. They are written in hieroglyphics and hieratic.

c THE VERNACULAR: in the earlier epochs only faintly traceable; generally used in daily intercourse and secular writings of the New Kingdom; written almost entirely in hieratic on papyrus. From this idiom the language of the Late Period was developed, which was written in demotic and used in official documents down to the Roman period.

COPTIC: spoken in Christian times, and also used for the translation of the Bible, etc. It is a development of the vernacular of earlier times, and is written with the Greek alphabet and native supplementary letters, and hence is known to us in vocalization also.

The Egyptian language is written in three different § 9.
styles of script, which in this introduction are always transposed into hieroglyphics, facing towards the left. All scripts render only the consonants, without considering the vowels.

HIEROGLYPHICS: used in temples and tombs *a*
carved in stone and wood or painted in colours; facing usually towards the right, but sometimes, for decorative reasons, towards the left. The knowledge of them was confined to priests and scholars.

HIERATIC: written on papyrus with a dried rush *b*
stem and black or red ink. The individual signs are written in more or less abbreviated form according to the hand-writing. They stand for hieroglyphs, and are always rendered in this introduction by hieroglyphs. They are written from right to left; but as hieroglyphics they are reversed in this introduction.

DEMOTIC: an abbreviated script (brachygraph) *c*
of the Graeco-Roman period developed from the Hieratic; facing towards the right.

The Script.

§ 10. The hieroglyphic script originated in pictures of visible objects; a picture was drawn and the name of the represented object, or the act indicated thereby, was pronounced. For example 𓁷 was written for *ḥor* "face", or 𓁹 for *yar(t)* "eye" and for words of "seeing". Later on, these pictures were also used for words which happened to be composed of the same consonants as those which made up their own name; thus 𓁷 was written also for *ḥir* "upon" and for *ḥray* "the upper", likewise 𓁹 was used for all forms of the verb "to make", *yir*, *yer*, *yor*, etc. In all these cases no account was taken of the vowels, so that gradually the original pictures of objects became signs for groups of consonants. Some of these groups of consonants were very short, and appeared in other words as syllables. Herein lies an important step in the evolution of hieroglyphics towards a phonetic script. Finally, some of the characters depreciated so much, that they represented only one consonant. It thereby became possible to write any desired word as well as to denote the grammatical endings of words.

§ 11. The hieroglyphic script of historical times contains elements of every epoch of its development; it has, in the first place, pictures for whole words ("word—signs"), or for small groups of consonants (wrongly called "syllabic-signs"); and secondly, alphabetic phonetic signs for individual consonants (§ 12). A very practical habit of the Egyptians helps us to obtain quickly and almost accurately the meaning of words written phonetically:

they placed at the end of almost every word a picture ("determinative" or "explanatory-sign"), by which they indicated the group to which the word in question belonged. The determinatives and word-signs are closely connected in origin and use. Thus, after names and designations of men is placed a , of women a , of gods a , of birds a , of snakes a ; after substantives and verbs which are associated with the idea of running a , with that of eating and speaking a , with that of seeing a , with that of sun, light, or time a , with that of a range of desert mountains a , with that of fire a ; after abstracts a parchment-roll ; after energetic activities a or etc.

The number of determinatives is very large, and for individual words they can be used and multiplied to almost any extent; yet in general, there are certain definite ways of writing the words; and, in fact, as time passed, more and more determinatives were placed after a word
(§ 12 on page 6; cf. p. *1). § 12.
Some characters were taken later on into the alphabet, § 13.
and, occasionally in the Middle Kingdom, but often in the New Kingdom, they occur instead of the older characters. They are for *m*, for *n*, for *y*, for *w*. Further, quite early they wrote instead of for *y* and or for *m*.

§ 12. LIST OF PHONETIC SIGNS (ALPHABET)

Name of the Sign[1]	Signs	Sound	Semitic[2]	Name of the Sign	Signs	Sound	Semitic
eagle		ꜣ	א	coil		ḥ	ח, ح
reed-leaf		y	י	disk		ḫ	ח, ج
arm		ʿ	ע	club		ẖ	ח, ح، خ
chicken		w	ו	bolt		s	ז
leg		b	ב	linen-band		ś	שׂ
box		p	פּ	pond		š	שׁ
snail		f	פ	triangle		ḳ	ק
owl		m	מ	basket with handles		k	כ
water		n	נ	stand		g	ג
mouth		r	ר	wall-top		t	ת
bend		h	ה, א	tongs		ṯ	ס
				hand		d	ט
				snake		ḏ	צ

[1] The designations are traditional and partly quite arbitrary; they may not at all mean what the picture represents.

[2] The Semitic equivalents are in reality more complicated than can be represented in this tabulated and preliminary list.

The Egyptians laid more stress on the calligraphy § 14.
than on the correct writing of a word. The characters belonging together were always placed in a square; thus

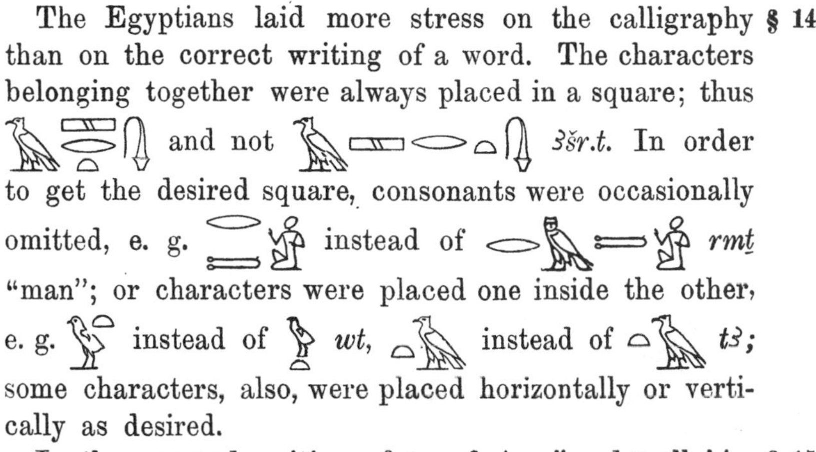

and not *ȝšr.t.* In order to get the desired square, consonants were occasionally omitted, e. g. instead of *rmṯ* "man"; or characters were placed one inside the other, e. g. instead of *wt,* instead of *tȝ;* some characters, also, were placed horizontally or vertically as desired.

In the use and writing of "word-signs" and "syllabic- § 15.
signs" (for words of more than one consonant) they proceeded quite differently, sometimes according to rule, sometimes at will and variably. Namely:

a) All consonants of syllabic-signs were, in addition, *a*
written out singly; e. g. *šbk* "crocodile", *ymȝḫ* "respectable", *mȝꜥ* "just".

b) Only the first consonant was written separately: *b*
wḏ "to command".

c) Only the last consonant was written separately: *c*
ḥtp "to rest", *ꜥnḫ* "to live"; syllables: *mn,* *mr.*

d) The word-sign, with or without a stroke under or *d*
after it, stands alone, without the addition of a consonant: *ḫrp* "guide", *pr* "house", *mr* "director", *ḥry* "chief".

§ 16. As in Semitic grammar, *y* and *w* are called "weak consonants". They are often not written even when they are spoken; perhaps because they had occasionally, as is certainly the case in Coptic as well as in Semitic languages, the value of a vowel ("half-vowel").

§ 17. The determinatives are added or omitted, often at will. The number of added determinatives, also, is not the same in different kinds of orthography; in general, papyri oftener than inscriptions have a determinative, and, indeed, since the New Kingdom, prefer several determinatives after a word. Examples: [hieroglyphs] or [hieroglyphs] *śn*, "brother", [hieroglyphs] *ꜥꜣ* "great", [hieroglyphs] *kꜣ.t* "work", [hieroglyphs] or [hieroglyphs] *wśyr* "Osiris", [hieroglyphs] *wn* "to open", [hieroglyphs] *wśtn* "to step".

§ 18. Special script-play arose, due to the fact that signs for holy or revered persons or things were placed before

a those signs which they should immediately have followed. Examples: [hieroglyphs] *ḥm-nṯr* "servant of the god, prophet", [hieroglyphs] *ḥ.t-nṯr*, "house of the god, temple", [hieroglyphs] *mry ymn* "beloved of Amon" (Μιαμοῦν).

b Names of kings were enclosed in an oblong, ("king's ring, cartouche") [hieroglyph] (hieroglyph for *rn* "name"). Examples: [hieroglyphs] *ymn-ḥtp* Amenhotep, [hieroglyphs] *ḏśr-kꜣ-rꜥ* (first name of Amenhotep I).

c Stereotyped formulas and frequently recurring titles were repeated only in recognized abbreviations. Examples: [hieroglyphs] *śtn byty* "king of Upper Egypt, king of Lower

Egypt"; [hieroglyphs] *kꜣ nḫt* "the strong ox" (king's title), [hieroglyphs] *ḥm-nṯr tpy* "first prophet, chief priest"; [hieroglyphs] *ʿnḫ, wḏꜣ, śnb*, "may he live, be happy and well" after the names of kings (*56, 1).

Our transcription in Latin letters is not meant to render every hieroglyphic character, but only the consonantal value (without repetition) which is represented; thus, we transcribe [hieroglyphs] not by *śn-n-man* but by *śn*. Furthermore, the omitted weak consonants *y* and *w* are also to be inserted in the transcription: [hieroglyphs] *ḳbḥw* „cool water". Finally, the old consonantal values which were altered because of the change of sound are to be replaced (§ 33). In each word, the root is separated by a point from the preceding and succeeding parts (*ś.ʿnḫ* "to give life", *m.śḏm.t* "rouge", *pr.f* "his house"); compound words are connected by a hyphen (*ḥm-nṯr* "servant of the god"). § 19.

Preliminary Survey.

The Egyptian has two genders: masculine and feminine. § 20.
Masculine substantives and adjectives have no ending which is invariably present; feminines add *t* to the stem: [hieroglyphs] *sꜣ* "son", [hieroglyphs] *sꜣ.t* "daughter"; [hieroglyphs] *sꜣ nfr* "a good son", [hieroglyphs] *sꜣ.t nfr.t* "a good daughter".

Substantives and adjectives can stand in:

Singular; ending: mas. —, fem. *t*. *a*

b Plural; ending: mas. *w*, fem. *wt*; always with the addition of three strokes ı ı ı or ⋮. Examples: *ḥꜥw* "the arms", *ḥm.wt* "the workshops". (Continued in § 36a.)

The definite article is *pꜣ* "the" (mascul.), *tꜣ* "the" (femin.), cf. examples in § 41.

§ 21. *a* The nominative and accusative are not differentiated in hieroglyphics; thus *śtn* "the king" (nom. and acc.); *św* "he" and "him".

b The addition of the preposition *n* corresponds to the English dative with "to"; thus *n śtn* "to the king."—Cf. § 61c.

c The genetive relation is rendered either by direct proximity of the two words ("status constructus" or "construct state"); or by means of the connecting word *n*, fem. *n.t*, plural or *n.w*, which agrees in gender and number with the preceding substantive. Examples: *mr mšꜥ* "commander of the army" (*2, 6); *pr n ymn* "house of Amon" (*2, 9); *šmꜥy.t n.t ymn* "dancing-girl of Amon" (*2, 10); *ḥmw.t n.w ḥ.t-nṯr* "workshops of the temple" (*2, 11). (The hieroglyphs of these examples should always be copied from the reading exercises.)

§ 22. As in Semitic languages, the pronoun can be affixed ("pronominal suffix") to the substantive with which it is intrinsically connected: *sꜣ.y* "my son", *pr.k* "thy house", *ḫ.t.f* "his body", *s3.t.ś* "her daughter".

§ 23. The same pronominal suffixes are attached to the root of the verb in order to indicate the subject. E. g. from *śdm* "to hear" we have the present: *śdm.y* "I hear", *śdm.k* "thou hearest", *śdm.f* "he hears", *śdm.śn* "they hear". In like manner the perfect, which attaches *n* as a sign of time to the stem of the verb: *śdm.n.y* "I have heard", *śdm.n.k* "thou hast heard", *śdm.n.f* "he has heard".

§ 24. As a preliminary to the subject of prepositions, note the following: *m* "in", "with"; *n* "for", *r* "to", *ḥr* "upon".

§ 25. The order of words in the Egyptian sentence is essentially the same as in the Semitic, this order being: 1) verb, 2) subject, 3) object, 4) further modifications.

§ 26. Models of verbal sentences:

a With a transitive verb: *rdy ḥ3.ty-c t3 n ḥkr* "the count gives bread to the hungry" (*3,5): *rdy.y n.k šfy.t.k m yb.w n.w rmṯ* "I give (place) thee thy reputation in the hearts of men" (*3,6).

b With an intransitive verb: *ḥtp ytm m y3ḫ.t ymn.ty.t* „Atum sets in the western horizon" (*3,7).

c With the verb "to be": *yw d3b ym f* "figs are in it" (*7,2).

§ 27. The verb "to be" can be omitted; in which case the sentence consists merely in a "noun" (substantive) and adjective, and is called a "nominal sentence". *ʿ3 by.t.f, ʿš3 b3k.w.f* "its honey (is) enormous, its olive-trees (are) innumerable" (*7,4).

§ 28. With regard to the attaching of subordinate sentences the following is important:

a Relative sentences are either not introduced at all, or are introduced by the connective *nty* "which, fem. *nty.t*, plu. *nty.w*. Examples: "the singer, *nty m t3 (m.)ʿḥʿ.t* who is in the grave" (*49,2).

b The negative *nn* "not" is used before negative nominal and verbal sentences; e. g. *nn ḏrw* "there is no limit" (*7,7); "a bark, *nn ḥm.ś* whose rudder was not there" (*43,4); *nn šnʿ.w b3.y* my soul was not guarded (*23,7).

Phonology.

The following should be added to the table (§ 12) of alphabetic signs and their meaning:

§ 29. *a* To the "weak" consonants: *3* is so closely related to the weak consonants that it is often not written; e. g. *ḏf3* "food". It sometimes changes to *y*, e. g. in *p3* "to fly"; in which case the word is often written with , as in the old orthography, still another *y* being added to the : *py*.

𓇋 *y* has a double nature; it corresponds in Coptic, as well as in the Semitic languages, sometimes to *y*, sometimes to *ꜣ*. As a weak consonant it is often not written (§ 16). It changes with 𓅱 *w* (cf. *d*). *b*

𓂝 *ʿ* is, in contradistinction to *ꜣ*, *y*, and *w* a strong and unchangeable consonant, which, until the fifth century B. C., was still spoken, and its influence appears in the Coptic etymology. *c*

𓅱 *w*, as a weak consonant, is often not written (§ 16). In some words old *w* becomes *y*, in others old *y* becomes *w*. *d*

§ 30. *a* As to *n*, *r*, *l*: the Egyptian script knows no *l*; where the Coptic has an *l*, or where the corresponding Semitic indicates it, *n* 𓈖 or 𓂋 *r* or the vulgar combination 𓈖𓂋 or 𓈖𓏥𓂋𓏤 *nr* is found.

b Final 𓂋 *r* sometimes appears in the script slurred to 𓇋 *y* (i. e. *ꜣ*?), and then in Coptic disappears. In reality it disappeared in early times. Such an *r* is written 𓂋𓇋, which can only be transcribed in an historical way by *r*, or by *y* according to the effected vowel-change. Cf. *św*r, *24,1; *śḳr* *13,5.

§ 31. The aspirates. They were sharply distinguished from each other in the older language. 𓉔 *h* somewhat as in our "have", 𓎛 *ḥ* as in the energetic shout "ha!", 𓐍 *ḫ* as in the Scotch "loch"; 𓄡 *ẖ* somewhat similar to the last, and was in part changed to 𓐍 *ḫ*.

§ 32. The *s* and *t* sounds:

a In the Middle Kingdom the *s* sounds, *s* and *ś* were interchangeable.

b Of the dentals, in the Middle Kingdom *ṯ* became *t* and *ḏ* became *d*. The Semitic equivalents are here especially complicated, and our traditional transcription certainly does not reproduce the spoken sound.

§ 33. The most frequent cases of sound-change are (§ 29—32):

a *ꜣ* and *r* to *y*.

b *y* to *w* and the reverse.

c *ẖ* to *ḫ*.

d *s* to *ś* and the reverse.

e *ṯ* to *t* and *ḏ* to *d*.

f All these transitions, in the designation of which the hieroglyphics are not consistent, had been made as early as the Middle Kingdom; hence, from this time on, for can be given an old *s* or *ś*, and for an old *t* or *ṯ* etc. From the beginning a habit should be formed of using the old signs *ẖ*, *s*, *ś*, *ṯ*, and *ḏ* in transcription, to impress upon the mind the original phonetic value, even when they are written with the hieroglyphics for more recent sounds.

g and are wrongly written where *t* and *d* respectively (not at all derived from *ṯ* and *ḏ*) are meant; e. g. *ś.nḏm.ṯ* instead of *ś.nḏm.t* *50,4; *yṯn* instead of *ytn* *23,5 *24,5. Likewise (which as a grammatical ending depreciated to *t*, § 81) for *t*.

Where in the course of centuries there arose trans- § 34.
positions in consonantal values, first of all there was written the original phonetic value with its peculiar word or syllable sign—just as in the case of the reproduction of a consonant, changed on account of a change in sound (§ 29a, 30b)—and then the transposed consonants were again added in their new position. Hence from the old *ḳmꜣ* "to create", arose the later *ḳꜣm* ; in like manner, out of *ymꜣ* "goodness", arose the later *yꜣm* .

Nouns.

The noun (substantive and adjective) has essentially § 35.
the following root forms:

With two, three or more consonants: among which *a*
may be "weak" ones, which are not always written.

Formations with an *m* prefixed to the root (just *b*
as in Semitic). Examples: *m.śḏm.t* "paint" from *śḏm* "to paint".

Compounds with prefixed *nt* or *bw* (really, *c*
"place") express abstracts, or with suffixed *yr.f* ("he does") express the names of professions and of attributes. Example: *bw-nfr* "the good".

d Some substantives, especially names of gods, have a singular ending in *w*, which is often not written; e. g. *Mntw*, *Jtmw*.

e Compounds often have a special determinative for the whole group; e. g. *r3-pr* "temple"; *nty.w-ym* "the dead" (*32,4).

§ 36. The plural endings are: masc. *w*, fem. *wt*. They are written:

a Either by writing the word sign three times, according to ancient custom: *nṯr.w* "gods".

b Or by a word sign with the "plural-strokes" (§20b): .

c Or by the "plural-strokes" after the determinative: .

d In all these cases the *w* of the ending in both genders is seldom written, e. g. (ancient).

§ 37. The "plural-strokes" often do not denote a real plural, but a singular word with a plural meaning. Examples:

a collectives: *yrp* "wine" (*7,3);

abstracts: *ḫcw* "splendour" (*4,7).

b Such words, even when they are written without the plural-strokes, are often constructed like a plural, having their verb in the plural; the same is true of compounds with *nb* "each". Example *5,7–8: "my milk (streams), *cšḳ.n* they enter thee".

§ 38. In compound words only the first part takes the plural ending; e. g. *ḥ3.tyw-c* "counts" from ḥ3.ty-c; ymy.w-bcḥ "forefathers" from ymy-bcḥ, r3.w-pr "temples" *31,10.

In addition to the plural, the old language had a dual, which in some cases lasted into the time of the Coptic. Ending: masc. *wy* fem. or *ty*. The dual was written: **§ 39.**

a a) by means of a repetition of the word sign: *c.wy* "both arms"; cf. *tḫn.wy* *16,6.

b b) by means of a repetition of the determinative: *rd.wy* "both feet", cf. *40,2. 43,5.

c c) by means of the addition of the "dual-strokes" \\; which are then taken as a sign for the ending *y*: *śn.ty* "both sisters". In like manner, the suffix of a dual noun can take the "dual-strokes": *ynḥ.wy.f* *46,9.

For extant Egyptian nouns with both genders (masculine and feminine) cf. § 20. Names of foreign lands are feminine, e. g. *k3š ḫsy.t* "the wretched Cush (Nubia)" *30,8. **§39A.** a

The neuter is represented: in antiquity by the feminine (cf. § 120), in more recent times by the masculine: cf. *yry.w* "that which is done (masc.)" *25,7. b

For the connection of two substantives with or without the connective *n* cf. § 21c. To indicate an attribute a substantive is joined to an adjective; e. g. *w3ḥ śtny.t* "fortunate in royalty" (*4,7). **§ 40.**

The classical language has no article. In the vernacular, the definite article "the" was developed from the demonstrative pronoun "this" *p3*, *t3*, **§ 41.**

n3 (§57d), and lasted into the classical period (§8b). Likewise, the indefinite article "a" was developed from the numeral [hieroglyphs] *wc* "one" (§46). Examples: *p3 t3* "the land" (*50,8); *t3 (m.)chc.t* "the grave" (*49,2); *n3 hr.w* "the wretched ones" (*52,9); *wc.t ssm.t* "a mare" (*40,11). —For declension cf. § 21.

Adjective

§ 42. In writing, adjectives are usually not distinguishable
a from substantives and participles. For adverbs cf. § 66.
b An especially frequent nominal formation in adjectives is the "gentilic", which is formed by the addition of [hieroglyphs] or \\ *y* to a substantive; it is also derived from prepositions: § 63. The ending *y* is often not written, especially in the feminine. Gentilic forms derived from feminine substantives end, in the singular: mas. [hieroglyphs] *ty*, fem. [hieroglyphs] or [hieroglyphs] *ty.t;* in the plural: mas. [hieroglyphs] *tyw*, fem. [hieroglyphs] *tyw.t*. Examples *hm.ty* "artist" (*2,2) from *hm.t* "art"; *nw.ty* "municipal" from *nw.t* "town", plural *nw.tyw* *21,11; *mh.ty* "northern" (*17,11) from *mh.t* "north".

§ 43. The adjective follows the substantive which it qualifies, and agrees with it in number and gender; the writing of the ending, however, is very irregular and careless. The adjective [hieroglyphs] *ky* "the other", fem. [hieroglyphs], *kty*, is exceptional in that it precedes its substantive; examples: *ky rmṯ* "another man"; *kty pẖr.t* "another remedy".

The adjective *ḏś* "self" with suffixes is used in a § 44. special way. Examples: *śtn ḏś.f* a "the king himself"; *ḫpš.y ḏś.y* "my own crescent sword" (in a speech by the king).

Two compound expressions for "all", "the whole", are b used with suffixes: *r ḏr* "up to the border" and *my ḳd* "commensurable with the circumference". Examples: *tȝr ḏr.f* "the whole land" (*11,1); *rȝ.w-pr my ḳd.śn* "the temple in its completeness".

Egyptian apparently has no special forms of comparison. § 45. The comparative is expressed by means of the preposition *r* "more than" (§ 61 b). Examples: *wr n.f yrp r mw* "great to him wine than water = he has more wine than water" (*7,3); *ˁšȝ śt r šˁ n wḏb* "they are more numerous than the sand of the sea-shore" (*37,3).

Numerals

The numerals may be used as substantives or adjectives; § 46. the feminine and plural endings, however, are very seldom written.

The numeral signs are almost always used; only with the lowest units occasionally the phonetic sign is also used. The phonetic values, which are partly conjectured only by means of combination, are:

1	I	*wᶜ*	6	III III	*św*	10	∩	*mḏ*
2	II	*śn.wy*	7	III IIII	*śfḫ*	20	∩∩	*ḏwt(?)*
3	III	*ḫmt*	8	IIII IIII	*ḫmn*	30	∩∩∩	*mᶜbꜣ*
4	II II	*fdw*	9	III III III	*pśḏ*	40	∩∩ ∩∩	*ḥmw*
5	II III	*dwꜣ*				50	∩∩ ∩∩∩	*dwꜣ(?)*

60	∩∩∩ ∩∩∩	*św(?)*	100	𓍢	*šꜣ.t*	100000	𓆐	*ḥfn*
70	∩∩∩ ∩∩∩∩	*ḥśf(?)*	200	𓍢𓍢	*šꜣ.ty*	1000000	𓁨	*ḥḥ*
80	∩∩∩∩ ∩∩∩∩	*ḫmnw*	1000	𓆼	*ḫꜣ*			
90	∩∩∩ ∩∩∩ ∩∩∩	*pśḏ.tw(?)*	10000	𓂭	*ḏbᶜ*			

§ 47. The ordinal numerals are derived from the cardinals by affixing *nw*. Example: *ḥm-nṯr śn.nw* "the second prophet" (*5,3). But 𓄫 or 𓁶𓊪𓏭 *tpy* "the first" (*5,3) is an exception. Fractions are indicated by prefixing 𓂋 *r*: 𓂋𓏽 *r-fdw* "a quarter"; but 𓐛 *gs* "a half" is an exception.

§ 48. Dates usually have the form: "year *(ḥꜣ.t-sp)* 1, month
a *(ybd?)* 1, —season, day *(śśw)* 1 during *(ḥr)* the sovereignty of king N". We are accustomed to number the months or to give them the names which they bore among the people, the names being derived from the feasts celebrated in them. They are:

ꜣḫ.t "Inundation"	*pr.t* "Spring" ("sprouts")	*šmw* "Summer"
1. Thoth.	5. Tybi.	9. Pachon.
2. Paophi.	6. Mechir.	10. Payni.
3. Hathyr.	7. Phamenoth.	11. Epiphi.
4. Choiak.	8. Pharmuthi.	12. Mesorê.

After the twelve months the five intercalary days are inserted (*ḥry.w rnp.t* "those above [beyond] the year"). The sign , "month 1" is often replaced by *tpy* "first"; and the day-number can be omitted from the first day of the month. b

Examples: *5,1. *8,4. *17,1. *18,4.

Pronouns

§ 49. The independent pronoun is found in two different forms: an older one which is still in use in the classical language, and a more recent one which appeared as early as the Old Kingdom. The suffixed pronoun (§ 52) has an unmistakable relationship with the older pronoun. The more recent seems to be composed of the older pronoun and a stem *nt*. Both forms are known to Semitic languages also, where, in the singular persons, now one and now the other form is used (§§ 50—51 also reflexive).

§§50, 51,52.

	§ 50 Older forms	§ 51 Younger forms	§ 52 Suffixes	
Sing.				
I	*wy*	*ynk*	*y*	my
thou	*ṯw*	*ntk*	*k*	thy
fem.	*ṯn*	*ntṯ*	*ṯ*	
he	*św*	*ntf*	*f*	his
she	*śy*	*ntś*	*ś*	hers
it	*śt*			
Plural				
we	*n*	*ynn*	*n*	our
you	*ṯn*	*ntṯn*	*ṯn*	your
they	*śn*	*ntśn*	*śn*	their

§ 53. The regular sound-change (§ 33) brought it about that from the Middle Kingdom on *t* in every case could be written instead of *ṯ;* in like manner instead of . The suffix *y* "my" was often not written; it was also possible to substitute for it , , , or , if a god, king, man, or woman was the speaker. Likewise, *wy* "I" was also written or only (* 39,6). Examples: *ynk byk yꜣḫ* "I am a useful servant" (*9,11); *sꜣ.y n ẖ.t.y* "my son of my body" (*5,4).

The above forms of the independent pronoun (pronomen absolutum) are used both for the nominative ("I") and for the accusative ("me"); the dative ("to me") is represented by the preposition *n* (§ 61c) with suffixes. The neuter "it" as suffix is usually expressed by means of 𓋴 *ś* (cf. § 39Ab). Examples: *ś.nḫn.y ṯw* "I bring thee up" (*5,5); *ḥsy wy ḥm.f ḥr.ś* "his majesty praises me on account of it" (*54,11); *ś.ś3y.n.y wy* "I satiated myself (*45,11). § 54.

Contrary to the usual order of words (§ 25), the pronoun and also the preposition *n* with suffix stand immediately after the verb, and hence before the subject and object. If the sentence has two pronouns dependent upon the verb, the dative precedes the accusative: *d.yn.y n.k rnp.wt* "I gave thee the years" (*5,9); *ḥsy.n wy nb.y* "my lord praised me" (*42,2); *wšb.n.y. n.f ś.t* "I answered to him it (I answered him concerning it)" (*47,8). § 55.

For the demonstrative pronoun there are many different forms, which may be used as substantives or adjectives. In general the initial consonant is characteristic: *p* for the masculine, *t* for the feminine, and *n* for the plural. § 57a-c contains the older forms. When used as adjectives they are all placed after the substantive. On the other hand, the more recent pronoun *p3* "this" (§ 57d), and the later article "the" (§ 41), are placed before the substantive.: in like manner also the more recent plural forms —connected for the most part with *n*—i.e. *nn* and *nw* (§ 57e). Examples: 𓉐𓏤𓊪𓈖 *pr pn* "this house", 𓉗𓏏𓉐𓏏𓈖 *ḥ.t tn* "this castle", 𓅯𓄿𓇓𓏏𓈖 *p3 śtn* "this king" *nn n ḫ3ś.tyw* "these barbarians" (*31,1. 37,7). § 56.

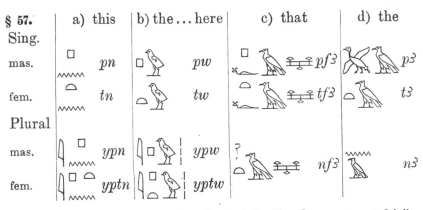

§ 57.	a) this	b) the ... here	c) that	d) the
Sing.				
mas.	*pn*	*pw*	*pfꜣ*	*pꜣ*
fem.	*tn*	*tw*	*tfꜣ*	*tꜣ*
Plural				
mas.	*ypn*	*ypw*	? *nfꜣ*	*nꜣ*
fem.	*yptn*	*yptw*		

e) More recent plurals (originally the neuter "this"): *nn*, *nw* "these".

§ 58. In short sentences, *pw* "thi3" is added for emphasis, where we are unable to reproduce it as a demonstrative pronoun. In verbal sentences it has hardly any significance, in nominal sentences it is used as a predicate or an nsertion (§131b). Examples: *ynwk pw* "I am it", *rn.y pw ḫnt nṯrw* "my name (is) at the head of the gods" (*39,2), *tꜣ pw nfr* "it is a beautiful land" (*7,1).

§ 59. The possessive pronouns of the Indo-Germanic languages ("my" etc.) were represented originally in classic Egyptian as in the older Semitic languages by suffixes (§ 52). The Egyptian vernacular, like the later Semitic dialects, devised later on a new form of possessive article. This is composed of the article (§ 57d) and suffixes (§ 52), and became more and more usual as time went on. The irregular writing is explained in §29a. Examples: *pr.f* or *py.f* (originated out of *p.ꜣf*) *pr* "his house".

Particles

PREPOSITIONS AND CONJUNCTIONS

Prepositions are divided into simple and compound, § 60.
according to their formation. They are sometimes combined with suffixes (§ 52), and used as conjunctions (§ 64a). Before suffixes they have occasionally a fuller writing, due to change of vocalization.

Simple prepositions (others are in the vocabulary): § 61.

m, with suffix *ym.f* "in him": in or a
out of a place; with persons or things; as an attribute (with "to be" § 131b). With infinitive "with" § 106.

r, with suffix *yr.f* "to him": towards some- b
thing or somebody; hostile to anyone; free from, hidden from something; more than something else (comparative § 45). With infinitive: in order to (§106).

n, with suffixes *n.f* "to him": for anyone c
(cf. dative § 21b); to anyone; on account of a matter. With infinitive: on account of, because.

ḥr; upon an object; on account of a matter. With d
infinitive: with, during (contemporaneous; §§ 106, 124b 125b, 132b).

ẖr: under an object, i. e. carrying it. e

ḫr: with a person; during the reign of (§ 48). f

yn: on the part of a person, through someone; g
used with the passive (§95—96) and to emphasize the subject (§131a), also with the infinitive (§ 107).

ḫnt before, at the head of. h

§ 62. Compound prepositions (to be found in the vocabulary under their chief constituent parts) consist mostly of a simple preposition and a substantive. The meaning of these phrases has gradually worn away. For example, compounds are made:

a With *m* "in": , *m-bꜣḥ* ("on the phallus of") "before" (*23,10. *29,9. *14,6); *m-ḥꜣ.t* ("at the head of") "before"; *šꜣꜥ-m* "since" *18,3; *m-ꜥ* "by" *54,5.

b With *n* "for": *n-mrw.t* ("out of love for") "on account of": *n mrw.t.k* "on account of thee" *12,7 (as conjunction: §64a).

c With *r* "to": *r-gś* ("at the side of") "near"; *ḥrw-r* ("distant from") "outside"; *nfry.t-r* "until"; "to" *18,4.

§ 63. Gentilic forms (cf. § 42b), the meaning of which often

a developed independently, were derived from the simple as well as the compound prepositions by using the suffix *y*. Examples: *ym.y* "he who is in or on something" from *m;* *yr.y* "he who belongs to someone, the companion" from *r;* *ḥr.y* "he who is upon something, the chief" from *ḥr;* *ḥry-yb* "dwelling in" from *ḥr.yb* "in the midst of".

b Gentilics are treated like adjectives or substantives, and take suffixes. Examples: *ym.y-yb n nṯr nfr* "darling (he who is in the heart) of the king" (*7,10); *ḥr.y-yb* *ȝbḏw, ḫnt.y ymn-tyw* "inhabitant of Abydos and director of the westerners" (*8,6-7); *ymy.t yb.k* "she dwells in thy heart" (*50,3); *ymy.w yw.w* "inhabitant of the island" (*13,8).

As conjunctions, use is made of either prepositions § 64.
(a) and other particles, which stand at the beginning of the sentence (b); or particles which are inserted as the second word in a sentence, and called enclitic conjunctions, because they were perhaps occasionally unaccented (c). In some sentences (§ 135, 138), there is, after the conjunctions, a verbal form corresponding to our "conjunctive" (§ 93). Among conjunctions, the following are especially frequent (others are in the vocabulary):

yr "if"; *m-ḫt* "after"; a
n-mrw.t "so that". Examples: *n-mrw.t mn rn.y* "that my name may endure" (*10,5), *n-ʿȝ.t-n mrr.y św* "because I love him" (*10,4), *m-ḫt śḏm.f ś.t* "after he had heard it" (*30,10), *r-nty.t kȝš wȝ.ty* "so that Nubia was inclined" (*30,8).

, *yśṯ* "since", "when"; , *ḥr* b
"since", "now", "but". Examples: *śṯ gm.n ḥm.y* "when my majesty had found him" (*25,5), *ḥr ptr yr.n.y śdm* "but then I heard" (*51,9).

śwt "but"; *yś* "how", "yes", "surely"; c
grt "but", "however", "further"; *gr* "also", "likewise", "but". Example: *yr gr.t rḫ rȝ pn* "but whoever knows this charm" (*56,9).

ADVERBS AND PARTICLES

§ 65. For adverbs, use is made either of invariable derivatives of substantives and adjectives (§ 66); or of particles which are connected with prepositions (§ 67). The particles usually stand at the beginning; in interrogative sentences (§ 137) also at the end of the sentence. Some are combined with suffixes (§ 69).

§ 66. The adverb derived from a noun is:

a apparently similar to it (the noun); occasionally with the ending *w* or *t:* *ḏ.t* "eternally", *nfr.w* "well", *wr.t* "very", "quite". Examples: *ꜣw yb.k my Rꜥ ḏ.t* "thy heart is glad as (that of) Re eternally" (*5,11), *wꜣś.y wr.t* "quite decayed" (*25,6; cf. *16,8), *ḫꜥy.k nfr* "thou shinest beautifully" (*55,1).

b is connected with a preposition, especially *r:* *r mnḫ* "in excellent manner"; *r yḫ.t nb.t* "above all" (*54,11), *r-my.ty.t* "in like manner" (*26,6).

§ 67. To the adverbs, which are derived from prepositions, belong:

a *ym* "there", "yonder"; *ḫnt* "before", "earlier". Example: *byk ym* "the servant here=I".

b *m-bꜣḥ* and *ḥr-ḥꜣ.t* "before", "formerly".

§ 68. Some adverbial particles stand in the second place in a sentence, e. g. *wy* "how", "pray". Examples:

ndm wy ym3.t.k "how beautiful is thy goodness" (*12,10), *yy wy* "come! welcome!" (*39,9).

Some particles which can only be rendered by an § 69.
adverb are combined with suffixes; their adaptability to different persons, however, has almost entirely disappeared, so that the particles were soon used unchangeably with one definite suffix. Some noteworthy ones are:

m "behold", later unchangeable *m.k* a
"behold (thou)", at the beginning of the sentence, often immediately before the subject.

, *yr* "but", "now", "namely", later unchan- b
geable *yr.f* as second word in a sentence: *hd.n yr.f t3 w3* "when the earth became bright in the morning" (*18,8).—*yr*, *yr.f* are used for emphasis after the imperative (§102), and in Interrogative sentences (§ 137).

The most frequently used interjections are: § 70.

y and *h3* "O!", "Ha!". They often stand a
before a proper noun, which is then preferably followed by *pn* "this": *y ʿnh.w* "O ye living!" (*21,5),

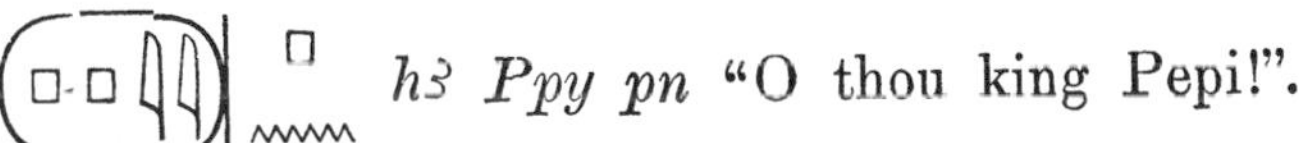

h3 Ppy pn "O thou king Pepi!".

In the Nominative of address, substantives often have b
the article: *p3 y.t-ntr* "O thou father of god" (*49,11), *p3 ytn* "O thou Aton!" (*55,2).

Some interjections have suffixes, e.g. *ynd-hr.k* "Hail, c
thou!" (*27,10. *31,8).

The Verb

THE ROOT OF THE VERB

§ 71. Verbs may be divided into the following groups according to the number and kind of the consonants of their root:

a) *Regular verbs.* These have two, three, four, or five "strong" consonants; the most frequent are those of three consonants. Examples: *mn* "to remain", *śḏm* "to hear", *wśṯn* "to invade", *nhmhm* "to roar".

§ 72. b) *Weak verbs.* These have three, four, or five consonants, of which the last is a weak one (*y* or *w* cf. § 16). Although the weak consonant was usually not written, it nevertheless influenced the formation of individual forms. It manifests itself especially in the feminine infinitive (§ 104), as well as in the possibility of doubling in the tense *śḏm.f* (§ 91) and in the participles (§ 113). Examples: *mśy* "to give birth to", *ḫnty* "to sail up stream".

§ 73. c) *Duplicating verbs.* These have three, four, or five consonants, of which the last two are alike. Often only one of these two consonants is written, from which it may be concluded that a double consonant was pronounced. Both consonants were written (evidently because a vowel was pronounced between them), not only as in the case of weak verbs in the accented form of tense *śḏm.f* (§ 91), and in the participles (§ 113), but also in other forms of the suffix conjugation, as well as in the qualitative (§ 80), in the infinitive (§ 104), in the imperative (§ 100), etc. The infinitive, contrary to the weak verbs, is always masculine (§ 104). Examples:

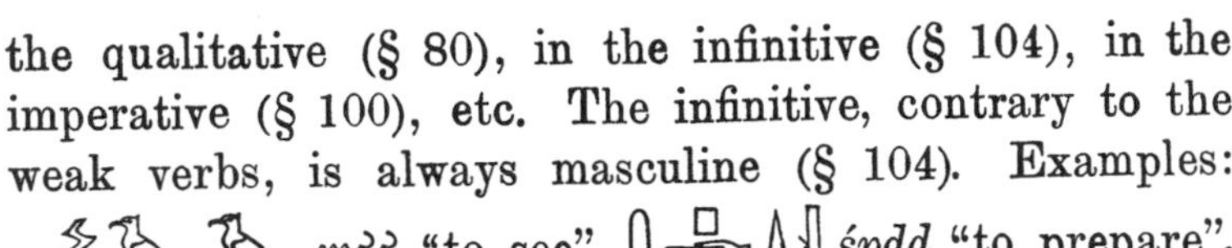

m33 "to see", *śpdd* "to prepare".

d) *Irregular verbs.* Some verbs appear written irregularly and occasionally differ from the forms of other verbs. Note:

1) Two verbs for "to give": , , *rdy* and § 74.
, , *dy;* both are weak verbs with feminine infinitive. The old language preserves almost all forms of both verbs; gradually *rdy* died out and was replaced by *dy*. The duplicating forms (§91) of *dy* were written , or , and read *dyy*.

2) Two verbs for "to come": *yy(y3y?)* and § 75.
, *yw(t);* both are weak verbs and have a feminine infinitive. The older verb *yw(t)*, which is used especially in dependent clauses, was gradually replaced by *yy*.

Among the numerous changes ("modifications, conju- § 76.
gations") of the root in Semitic languages, the following are frequent in Egyptian: the causative (§ 78) is formed by prefixing *ś* (Semitic *s* or *3*). The Piʿel formations with doubled middle consonant, which in Coptic have still to a certain extent an unusual vocalization, are not to be discerned in hieroglyphics; but yet, on account of the diversity of meaning in some verbs, they are to be

conjectured (e. g. *ẖny* "to sail" and "to convey anyone").

§ 77. Remains of other derivatives of a root are the forms with prefixed *n* like the Niphʿal (e. g. *nḏdḏd* "to endure" from *ḏd* "to endure"; with double final consonant like the Paʿlel (e. g. *śpdd* "to prepare"); with repetition of the last consonant like the "Palpel" and the "Paʿalʿel" (e. g. *śḫśḫ* "to hasten" (*41,2); *śdꜣdꜣ* "to tremble").

§ 78. The causatives (§ 76) are in general treated like verbs with the same number of strong or weak consonants; that is, causatives of three consonants like four-consonant verbs (e. g. *ś.nḫn* "to bring up" from *nḫn* "to be a child"). However, the causatives of two consonants have by way of exception a feminine infinitive. Example: Infinitive *ś.mn.t* from *ś.mn* "to establish", causative of *mn* "to remain".

§ 79. Apart from the infinitive, imperative, and the participles, only the perfect of the tense-formations (of Semitic languages) is preserved in the Egyptian conditional (§ 80). The imperfect has been replaced by the suffix conjugation (§ 83). The use of all Egyptian tenseforms was gradually limited by means of different combinations with auxiliary verbs (§ 121). Real moods are not traceable; forms which are used like our subjunctive appear in the tense *śḏm.f* (§ 91) and in the predicate (§ 97).

THE CONDITIONAL

(Called qualitative or pseudo-participle)

The endings (§ 81) are attached to the root; the *y* § 80.
and *w* occurring in them are often not written. In weak verbs (§ 72) the final weak root consonant *y* or *w* is usually not written. In duplicating verbs (§ 73) in earlier times the last consonant was occasionally doubled; later, however, this was hardly ever the case.

The endings of the conditional form (in parenthesis § 81.
are the later ones—that is, the forms developed by phonetic changes): the dual and the third plural died out early; they were replaced by the third masculine singular.

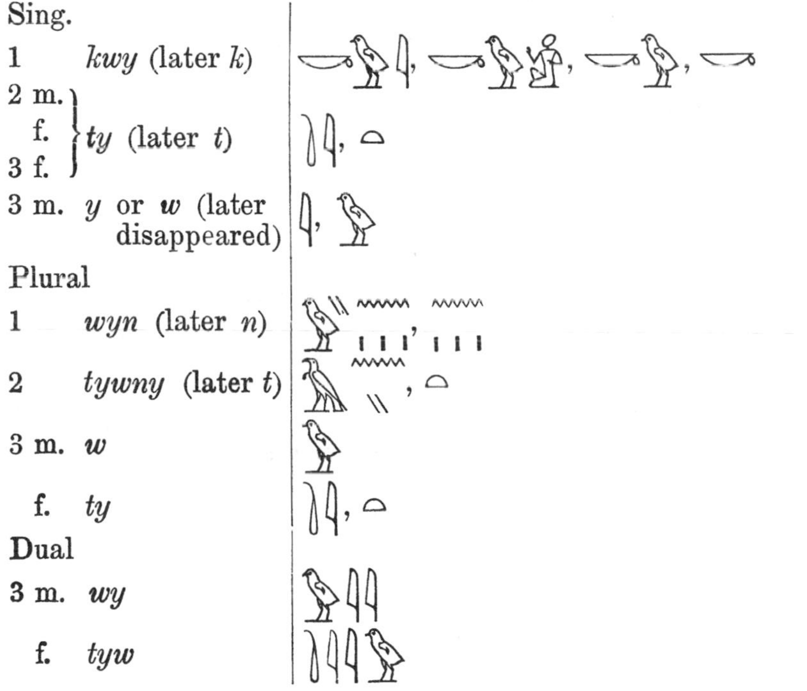

Sing.

1 *kwy* (later *k*)

2 m., f., 3 f. *ty* (later *t*)

3 m. *y* or *w* (later disappeared)

Plural

1 *wyn* (later *n*)

2 *tywny* (later *t*)

3 m. *w*

f. *ty*

Dual

3 m. *wy*

f. *tyw*

82. A transitive-active kind of conditional form, which was already rare in the older language, is found later, though only with *rḫ* "to understand", "to know", "to be able"; otherwise it always had an intransitive-passive meaning and indicated a conditional ("qualitative"). If it stands independently, as it also did (though rarely) in ancient times, it usually introduces the fulfilled condition of a previously mentioned action (apodosis). Usually it introduces a conditional sentence, which is subordinate to another sentence. Then it is often dependent on a verb which is in the tense of the suffix conjugation (§ 83), and thus resembles a participle ("pseudo-participle"). Cf. §§ 124a, 125a, 132a.

Examples: *yy.ty n.y ḥꜥty* "thou comest to me while thou rejoicest" (*12,5), *ywꜥ.kwy m nb* "I was rewarded with the gold" (*26,4), *wꜣḥ.f wy wḏꜣ.kwy* "he laid me down when I was healed" (*47,5).

THE SUFFIX CONJUGATION

§ 83. The most frequent tenses (tempora) are formed by the addition of the suffixes (§ 52), either directly to the stem (*śḏm.f* tense) or after the insertion of syllables *(n, yn, ḫr, k)*, which are derived from particles (§ 84). From all these forms a passive (§ 95) can be built by the further insertion of the syllable *tw;* another form is the more comprehensive passive *śḏm.w.f* (§ 96). Further, from the tenses *śḏm.f* and *śḏm.n.f* substantival forms introducing relative sentences (§ 118) are built.

The tenses of the regular verb: The translations merely § 84.
define in a practical way, and by no means exhaust the meaning of individual forms.

Active	Passive
 *śḏm.f* he hears	 *śḏm.tw.f* he is heard
 *śḏm.n.f* he has heard	 *śḏm.n.tw.f* he has been heard
 *śḏm.yn.f* then he heard	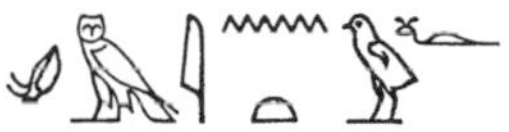 *śḏm.yn.tw.f* then he has been heard
 *śḏm.ḫr.f* he shall hear	 *śḏm.ḫr.tw.f* he shall be heard
 *śḏm.kȝ.f* thus he hears	 *śḏm.kȝ.tw.f* thus he is heard

Passive  *śḏm.w.f* (of *śḏm.f* and *śḏm.n.f*): "he is heard" and "he has been heard" (§ 96).

The inflection of tenses: If the subject is a noun, § 85.
it comes immediately after the root of the verb; e.g. *mn rn.y* "my name prospers" (*10,5), *ȝw yb.k* "may thy heart be glad" (*5,11). *yr.n ḥm.y nn* "my majesty did these things" (*10,3).

If the subject is a pronoun, it is added in the form § 86.
of a suffix (§ 52) to the root of the verb; the tense *śḏm.f* "he hears" is perhaps built on the form of a noun

("his hearing"). According to the Coptic the pronounciation was something like *śedmóf*.

§ 87. Almost all tenses can also be impersonally used in the active and passive. Their appearance is then the same as before the nominal subject: *yy.tw* "one came" (*30,7), *yr.n.tw* "it shall be done" (*36,2), *rdy.tw m-ḥr-n ṯ3ty* "it was imposed upon the vizier (*52,4).

§ 88. The tense *śḏm.f* occurs in both independent and dependent sentences, for the past as well as for the present. It is used in assertions, questions, and direct and indirect speech, as well as in requests, and especially after verbs of causing, seeing, finding, etc., to express a condition, purpose, or result. Examples: *wn n.k p.t* "the heaven is open for thee" (*6,1), *nḫn.y r bw ẖr ḥm.f* "I grew up at the residence of the king" (*10,2), *dy.y m3.śn ḥm.k* "I charge that they see thy majesty" (*13,6), *dy.śn pr.t-r-ḫrw* "may they (the gods) give a funerary offering" (*8,8; 22,4).

§ 89. The tense *śḏm.n.f* indicates the past, and is used in a manner similar to *śḏm.f*. It often appears independently in historical narrative, besides like a pluperfect dependent upon *m-ḫt* "after (he had heard)". Example: *šmś.n.y nṯr nfr* "I have served the king (*9,10).

§ 90. In the same way the tense *śḏm.yn.f* often appears in the historical narrative; while *śḏm.k3.f* usually appears in the conclusion of conditional sentences. Both *śḏm.yn.f* and *śḏm.k3.f* as well as *śḏm.ḫr.f* often express also a command. Example: *ḫᶜ.yn ḥm.f* "his majesty appeared" (*30,9).

§ 91. The weak and duplicating verbs (§ 72,73) show in the tense *śḏm.f* two different moods (manner of speech), which in the strong verbs we cannot satisfactorily ascertain, probably owing to our ignorance of vocalization.

The two moods are

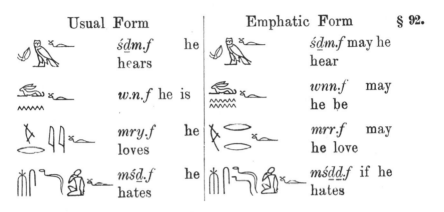

Usual Form		Emphatic Form		§ 92.
	śḏm.f he hears		*śḏm.f* may he hear	
	w.n.f he is		*wnn.f* may he be	
	mry.f he loves		*mrr.f* may he love	
	mśḏ.f he hates		*mśḏḏ.f* if he hates	

The emphatic form is often used independently, and § 93.
dependently (but not regularly) where special stress is laid on the verb; thus in sentences of wish, condition, question, precept, threat, consequence, etc., whether they are introduced by a conjunction or not. It is also used in sentences of temporal subordination and in emphatic phrases. The emphatic is to be translated sometimes like a conjunctive; but usually, however, not differently from the simple form of the verb.

The emphatic (doubled) form is frequent only in the § 94.
active *śḏm.f*. It is also found, however, in the passive, *śḏm.tw.f*. In the other tenses of the suffix conjugation it is not found at all. Examples: *n-ꜥ3.t-n mrr.y św* "because I certainly love him" (*10,4), *mrr.ṯn* "if you

wish" (*21,9), "I hid myself for fear, *mꜣꜣ wršy.t* the guard should see (me)" (*43,6), "he who desires *ḥss św ḫnty ymn.tyw* that the First of the Westerners praise him" (*21,1).

§ 95. In the passive of the suffix conjugation, the following differences occur:

a) The passives, which according to the table in § 84 form almost every tense by means of *-tw*, are closely related, even in meaning, to the active, from which they are derived; *ʿš.tw wr.w m-bꜣḥ* "the great ones were called before (his majesty)" (51,5), *drp.tw.f* "may he be presented with offerings" (23,8), *gm.n.tw Ḥr* "Horus was found" (*33,11).

§ 96. b) The passive *śḏm.w.f* (Table § 84 end) has the ending *w* in the singular, and *y* in the plural; neither of them are ordinarily written. The duplicating verbs show the doubling; the weak verbs often do not have the last weak consonant and the ending *w* written. Examples: *n sp yry.w myty.t* "never was the like done" (*16,10), *rdy.w n.f yꜣw.t* "the office was given to him" (*34,1 between *śḏm.n.f* forms).

PREDICATIVE

§ 97. An old form, whose use is confined to a few definite cases, is still seen in the so-called predicative. It has the ending *w* which is often not written; before this the duplicating verbs show the doubling, and the weak verbs usually do not write the last weak consonant *y*. The predicative is unchangeable, without regard to the gender, number, and person of its subject; and it does not take a suffix. It is, therefore, followed either by a substantive or an independent pronoun.

The predicative is used only in negative sentences after the verbs *tm* and *ymy* "not to be", and usually has an active meaning: *r3 n tm wnm N* "charm for the not-to-be-eaten of N=charm that N be not eaten" (*56,8), *tm rdy ḥr gś* "who does not bend (the right) to the side" (*11,3). Cf. the prohibition § 103. **§ 98.**

IMPERATIVE

The imperative has a singular and a plural; a difference in gender is not distinguishable in hieroglyphics, but according to the Coptic it is assumed in vocalization. The singular shows the simple root of the verb; in the duplicating verbs it has the doubling. The plural has the ending *y* (later also *w*), which is often not written out, and which in the weak verbs merges in the last weak consonant. Usually the plural-strokes are added to the determinative. **§ 99.**

§ 100.

Singular
Plural
śḏm hear!
śḏm.y hear!
m33 see!
d3y.y cross over!

Examples: *ṯs ṯw* "lift up thyself" (*29,4), *yry hrw nfr* "make (celebrate) a beautiful day!" (*49,11. 50,9).

The following verbs have an irregular imperative: **§ 101.**

Verbs of giving (§74): , *ymy* "give!", *a ymy ḳmy r fnḏ.k* "place ointment on thy nose!" (*50,1), *b* Verbs of coming (§ 75): , *myw* "come!", , *my.y* "come ye!".

§ 102. To strengthen the imperative, an independent pronoun is often added: also the particle , *yr* (§69b), or the preposition *n* (§ 61b), both with suffixes: *ꜥḥꜥ yr.k* "stand up, thou!" (*38,4), *šsp n.k ḥtp-nṯr* "take to thyself the divine offering!"

§ 103. The negative of the imperative (the prohibition) is expressed by the imperative *ymy* "be not" with a following predicate (§ 98): *ymy śnḏ* "fear not!" (*48,7).

INFINITIVE

§ 104. The infinitive is sometimes treated as a verb, sometimes as a substantive. In strong verbs, its form is that of the simple root; in the duplicating verbs, it doubles the last consonant; the weak verbs and the causative of two consonant verbs (§ 78) take the feminine ending *t* as suffix. Table for the formation of the infinitive:

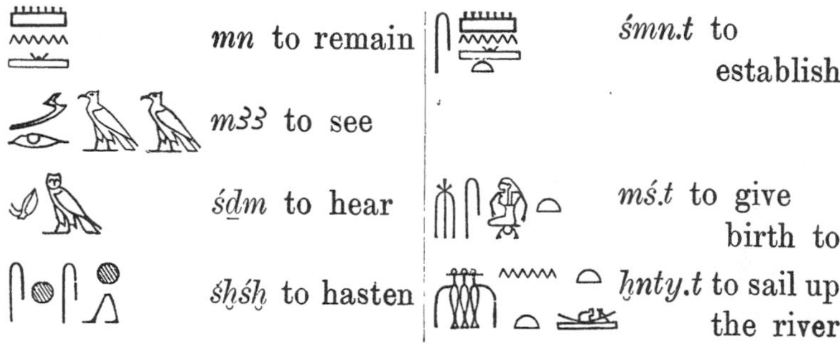

mn to remain	*śmn.t* to establish
mꜣꜣ to see	
śḏm to hear	*mś.t* to give birth to
šḫšḫ to hasten	*ḫnty.t* to sail up the river

The infinitive stands like a substantive, and is often **§ 105.**
not distinguishable from a real substantive (in *12,8 it
is even written as a plural):

a) In independent sentences as subject, object, predicate,
in the genitive, etc. Examples: "O ye living ones, *mrr.yw*
ꜥnḫ mśḏḏ.w ḫp.t who love life and hate death" (*36,4),
sp n hdhd "the time (example) of attack" (*37,6), *dy.y*
n.k ḳny.t "I give to thee to be strong (strength)" (*13,1).
"thy heart will be glad *n mꜣꜣ* on account of the sight"
(*56,4).

b) In sentences dependent upon verbs (especially **§ 106.**
commands, cause etc.) and prepositions such as *r*
"in order to", *m* and *ḥr* "with", "during" (simultaneousness, cf. §61). Examples: Osiris *dy.f* "may he give"
—*yr.t*—*śḫm*—*pr.t* "to do, to be powerful, to go out"
(*23,2—4). "I have brought thee up, *r ḥḳꜣ pḏ.t pśḏ* to
rule the nine bow-people" (*16,2). "Darling of the king
m ś.mnḫ mnw.f through the beautifying of his monuments"
(*27,2), *ẖ.wt ḥr sby.t* "bodies pass away" (49,6).

The logical subject follows the infinitive either in the **§ 107.**
genitive with *n* (§ 21c) or is introduced by the preposition *yn* "on the part of" (§ 61g). Example:
dwꜣ Wśyr yn N. "worship of Osiris by N." (*27,1. *31,6).

If the object is a substantive it follows immediately **§ 108.**
after the infinitive, if it is a pronoun it is added to the
infinitive as a suffix. Examples: „thou rejoicest *mꜣꜣ*
nfrw.y to see my beauty—the sight of my beauty (*12,5),
dwꜣ.f "to adore him" (*32,3).

An infinitive, independent and without the statement **§ 109.**
of a subject, often occurs in successive sentences, where

we should expect a verb. Example: *yr.t n.f śb3* "and he made a door for him" (*11,10. *12,3; likewise *śꜥḥꜥ* *16,6).

§ 110. The infinitive can be added to a verb of the same root as itself, as a complementary infinitive, for the purpose of strengthening. In such a case it has in general the usual form, although in three-consonant verbs it is feminine. Examples: *śḏm śḏm.t wꜥ* "who alone may listen" (*11,2), *ẖnn.śn ẖn.t* "if they row zealously" (*56,4).

§ 111. Closely related to the infinitive is a circumstantial form *śḏm.t.f* which looks like a feminine infinitive. In it the root of the duplicating verbs shows no doubling, and the weak consonants of the weak verbs are often not written. To express the subject it is combined either with a substantive which immediately follows the circumstantial form like a genitive, or with the pronominal suffix. The object, if it is a pronoun, follows the circumstantial form in the independent forms; in this it differs from the infinitive, which takes the suffix. At the beginning of a sentence or paragraph, the circumstantial form occasionally stands independently like a verb; often it comes after prepositions; often it indicates a temporal subordination. Example: *rdy.t.y w3.t n rdwy.y* "I gave my feet the way = ran on" (*43,5), *ḏr ḫpr.t mny* "since the death" (*39,10).

PARTICIPLES

§ 112. Participles are divided on the one hand into active and passive, on the other hand into complete (perfect) and incomplete (imperfect) action. In all participles, the root of the duplicating verbs can show the doubling; the root of the weak verbs shows it only in the imperfect participles. Table:

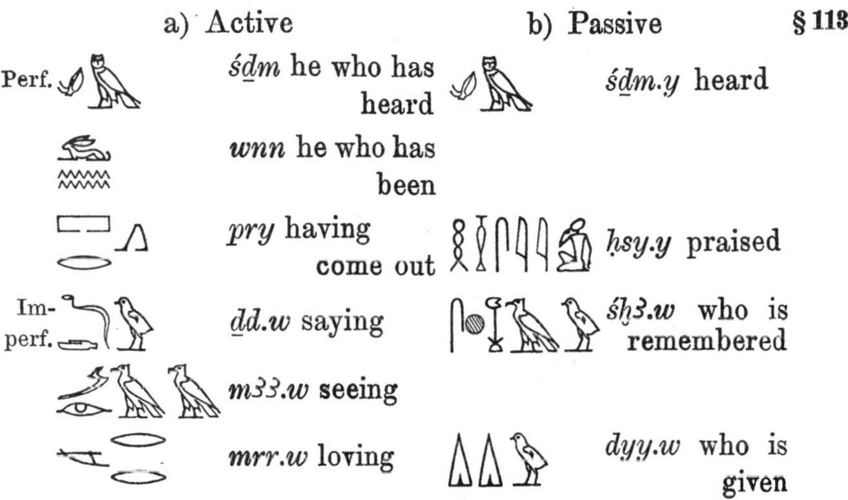

	a) Active	b) Passive	§ 113.
Perf.	*śḏm* he who has heard	*śḏm.y* heard	
	wnn he who has been		
	pry having come out	*ḥsy.y* praised	
Imperf.	*ḏd.w* saying	*śḫ3.w* who is remembered	
	m33.w seeing		
	mrr.w loving	*dyy.w* who is given	

The endings of the participles, as shown in the table, are, in the perfect: active —, passive *y*; in the imperfect: active *w*, passive *w*. In number and gender, the participles are like the noun; they take, therefore, in the feminine singular the ending *t*, in the plural, the plural-strokes and the ending *w*, feminine *wt*, although the *w* is not generally written. **§ 114.**

Examples: *mk km.t, wᶜf ḫ3s.wt* "who protects Egypt and subdues the foreigners" (*14,1, cf. *6,5), *mrr.w* "he who desires, that—" (*21,1), "his father *rnn św* who brought him up" (*25,9), *mḥ-yb* "he who fills the heart = darling" (*10,1), *ḥsy.y* "the praised" (*14,9), *d3w.w* "he who is honoured" (*32,1).

§ 115. The logical subject of passive participles is introduced either directly, or by *n*: *mry Rʿ, mś n Ḏḥwty* "beloved of Re, created by Thot" (*15,7). In genealogies: *yry n* "begotten by (chiefly of the father)" and *mśy n* "born of (mother)" (*21,4. *24,3).

§ 116. A rare participle with future meaning is found in the so-called verbal adjective: *śḏm.tyfy* "he who will hear"; in such a case the root of a duplicating verb shows the doubling, and the weak consonant of a weak verb is seldom written. Endings:

Sing. m.	*tyfy*	fem.	*tyśy*
Plur. m.	*tywśn*	fem.	*tywśt*

Examples: *śnb.tyfy* "he who will be well" (as proper noun: *15,3), "he who desires, *ḏd.tyfy* shall say" (*21,2), "each living one, *śwꜣ.tyfy* who will pass by" (*21,8).

§ 117. Another rare participle (*śḏm.n* "audible" indicates possibility. It occurs in only one form, which can take both the feminine and the plural ending (as § 114).

THE RELATIVE FORMS

§ 118. From the tenses *śḏmf* and *śḏm.n.f* of the suffix conjugation, substantival relative forms are derived, which take the masculine ending *w* (usually not written) or the feminine *t*, according as they refer to a masculine or feminine substantive. The verb root has in the form *śḏm.w.f* the same appearance as in the accented form of the *śḏm.f* (§ 92); hence the weak and the duplicating verbs have the doubling of the last strong consonants. Table of the relative forms:

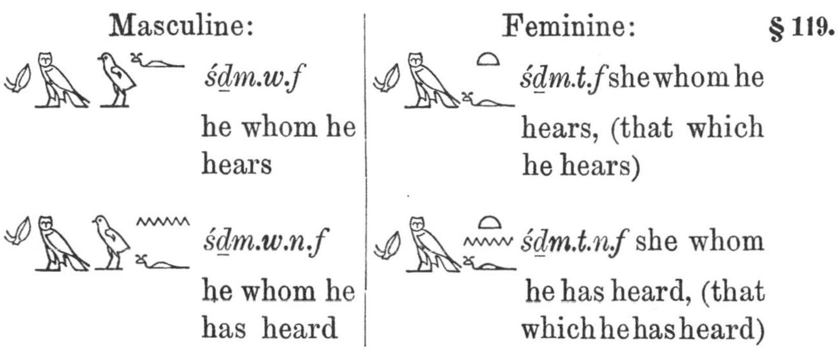

Masculine:		Feminine:	§ 119.
	śdm.w.f he whom he hears		*śdm.t.f* she whom he hears, (that which he hears)
	śdm.w.n.f he whom he has heard		*śdm.t.n.f* she whom he has heard, (that which he has heard)

The relative forms, which in use are with difficulty § 120.
differentiated from participles, are often used substantively. They can then be used with an adjective, especially *nb* "all". They usually introduce a relative sentence, e. g. in the enumeration of epithets. Examples: *dyy.t p.t, km3.t t3, ynn.t ḥ'py* "that which heaven gives, the earth creates, and the Nile brings" (*22,6), *nn yry.w.n.k n.y* "this which thou hast done to me" (*24,10), *šnn.t ytn* "that around which the sun revolves" (*24,5).

PERIPHRASTIC TENSES

The verb-forms are strengthened by many combinations § 121.
with auxiliary verbs; in the vernacular (§ 8c) these combinations, mostly with "to be" and "to make", gradually supplanted the simple verbforms of the older classical language.

The auxiliary verb "to be".

Some of the most frequent verb forms are strengthened § 122.

or paraphrased by prefixing the auxiliary [hieroglyphs] *yw* and [hieroglyphs] *wn* "to be". For the forms of the suffix conjugation (§ 83) two possibilities present themselves:

a When the subject occurs once:

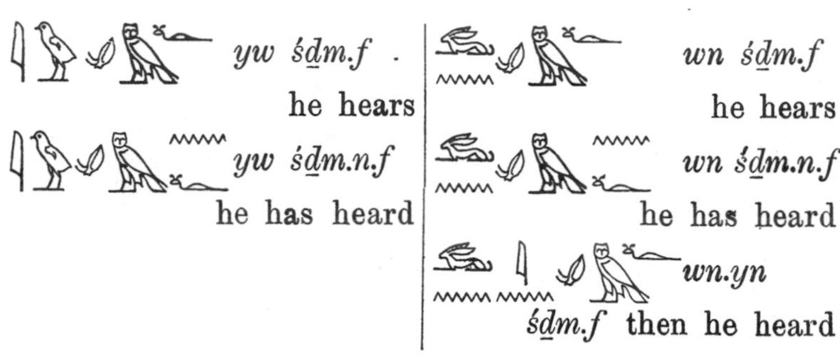

b When the subject occurs twice:

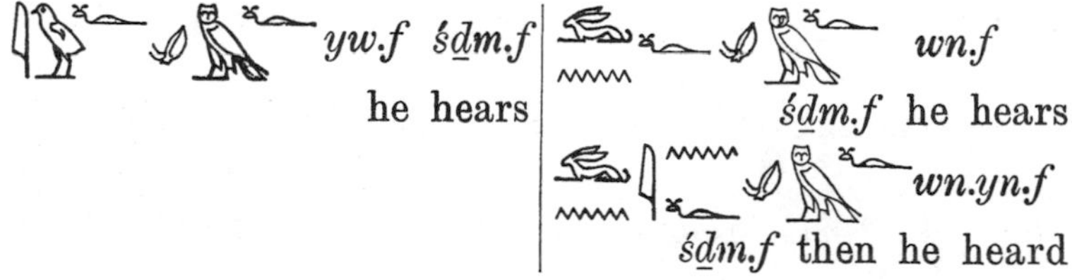

yw.f śḏm.f
he hears
wn.f śḏm.f he hears
wn.yn.f śḏm.f then he heard

§ 123. The verbs *yw* and *wn* "to be" can also be used before a genuine nominal sentence (§ 27). *yw ʿb.wy.ś m ḏ3ḏ3.k* "her horns are on thy head" (*38,8).

§ 124. In like manner those sentences which are not genuine nominal sentences (§ 132) can be introduced by *yw* or *wn:*

a With the qualitative (§ 80): *yw ṯ3 mdw* "the chicken is speaking = chirps" (*55,7).

With *ḥr* and the infinitive (§ 106): *yw bw-nb ḥr dwꜣ* b
nfrw.f "everyone praised his beauty" (*35,2; cf. *30,11-*31,1).

If the subject of these unreal nominal sentences is a **§ 125.**
pronoun, the following combinations present themselves, which are used very often in the vernacular of the New Kingdom (§ 8c) and which still continue in the Coptic:

With the qualitative: *yw.f śḏm.w* a
"he is hearing", *yw.k wbn.ty* "thou risest" (*55,3).

With *ḥr* and the infinitive: *yw.f ḥr* b
śḏm "he is hearing", *wn.yn.śn ḥr bhꜣ* "then were they by fleeing = then they fled headlong" (*37,9).

The future tense and the future command are ren- **§ 126.**
dered by the preposition *r* with the infinitive (§ 106); a
this occurs after the auxiliary verb *yw* "to be": *yw.ṯn r drp n.y* "ye shall sacrifice to me" (*36,7), *yw dp.t r yy.t* "a ship will come" (*48,8).

In an unreal nominal sentence (§ 132): *yb n ḥm.k r* b
ḳbb "the heart of thy majesty will be glad" (*56,3).

The auxiliary verb *ꜥḥꜥ* "to stand" is placed **§ 127.**
before a verb in order to reproduce the accentuation in historical narration. It appears usually as the tense *śḏm.n.f* *ꜥḥꜥ.n*, more seldom as *śḏm.f*: *ꜥḥꜥ*.

With forms of the suffix conjugation: *ꜥḥꜥ.n ṯḥn.n ḥm.f* a
ḥnꜥ.śn "then his majesty came into conflict with them" (*37,5).

With the qualitative (§ 80): *ʿḥʿ.n rdy.kwy r yw* "then was I thrown on the island" (*45,2).

§ 128. The auxiliary verb *yry* "to do" is used, in forms of the suffix conjugation, to paraphrase the respective forms of other verbs:

a First of all with compound verbs: *yry.ś dy-ʿnḫ* "may she be presented with life" (*12,4. *11,11).

b Then also with others: *yry.y šm.t* "I did the going = I went" (*43,8), *yry.n.y śḏm* "I learned" (*51,9); *yr.k ʿnḫ.ty* "mayest thou live" (*39,4).

§ 129. For historical narrative, especially with verbs of going, the combination of an infinitive with *pw* "this" and *yry.n.f* "he did" is used: *šm.t pw yry.n.f* "to go was that which he did = he went".

§ 130. The auxiliary verb *p3* "to have been", "to have had", in different verb forms is constructed, especially in negative sentences, with the infinitive of a verb, in order to denote a condition or an action which occurred in the past: *n sp p3.tw yr.t myty.t* "never was the like done" (*54,7).

Syntax

ORDER OF WORDS AND EMPHASIS IN PRINCIPAL SENTENCES

§ 131. The regular word-order in verbal and nominal sen-
a tences has already been discussed (§ 25-27). The word-order becomes irregular by emphasizing a word. The emphasized word is usually found at the beginning of a sentence and is introduced by the preposition *yn*

or *yr* . . . *yn ḥm.f rdy.f*———
"his majesty it was who gave———", *yr grt rḫ r3 pn*
"but whoever knows this charm" (*56,9).

In nominal sentences, which as a rule begin with the *b*
subject, the verb "to be" is to be understood (§ 27)
between the subject and the predicate. Often the pronoun
pw "this" (§ 57b, § 58) is inserted there. The predicate
may be introduced by *m* "as": *yb.y m śnw.y* "my
heart (was) my companion" (*45,5); *t3 nb m kśj.w* "Every
land was bowed" (*19,2).

The word-order, subject—predicate, of the nominal **§ 132.**
sentence (§ 27) is also transferred to sentences with
verb-forms (unreal nominal sentences). In such the verb
stands:

In the qualitative, especially with transitive verbs, to *a*
indicate a condition: *yb.w nḏm* "hearts were glad"
(*34,11), *d3d3.t hr.ty* "the council (of gods) was satisfied"
(*35,11), *śt cḥc.w ḥ3 ḳdš* "they are stationed behind
Kadesh" (52,3).

In the infinitive with *ḥr*, especially with transitive *b*
verbs, to indicate the beginning of a condition. Examples:
rḫy.t ḥr hy hnw "mankind began to rejoice and shout"
(*31,2), *pśḏ.t ḥr dw3.f* "the nine-fold (gods) praised him",
(*32,3).

These sentences can be introduced by an auxiliary *c*
verb "to be" (§ 124).

The omission of words is frequent in all kinds of **§ 133.**
sentences, especially in comparisons. Often the subject
or object is omitted, especially when it is a pronoun;
and likewise when the discourse is about the king. Cf.

also the impersonal use of the verbal forms (§ 87) and of the infinitive (§ 109). Examples: *ꜣw yb.k my Rꜥ* "thy heart be glad like (that of) Re" (*5,11), *yry.n.f m mnw.f* "he made (it) as his monument" (*6,8. *11,9. *12,2), *yry n.f N* "N makes (it) for him" (*6,11. *16,11). *ꜥš.tw wr.w m-bꜣḥ* "the princes were called into the presence of (his majesty)" (*51,5); *mnḫ.f ḥr yb* "he was pleasant to the heart (of the king)" (*27,7).

SPECIAL KINDS OF SENTENCES

Temporal sentences.

§ 134. The dependent temporal sentences are sometimes placed before, sometimes after the principal sentence. Usually they have no conjunction, so that the condition of dependence is shown only by the context and verb-forms. Occasionally they are introduced by *m-ḫt* "afterwards" (*30,10), *tp-ꜥ* "before" (*44,10), *ḏr* "since" (39,10) &c.

Examples: *yw wp.n.f—, yw.y ḥr ẖ.t.y* "he opened—, (while) I was on my belly" (*46,10-11), *ḏꜥ pr, yw.n m wꜣḏ-wr* "a storm arose, (as) we were on the sea" (*44,9. (*48,3), *ḥḏ.n tꜣ, pḥ.n.y* "when the earth had become light I arrived" (*43.9), *ḫft śpr ḥm.f r nhrn* "when his majesty came to Naharin (Mesopotamia)" (*40,4).

Conditional sentences.

§ 135. The conditional sentences can be introduced by *yr* "if"; often, however, there is no conjunction. The verb is usually found in a form of the suffix conjugation;

with the tense *śḏm.f* often in the accented form (§ 91): *ḥtp.k* "when thou settest, the earth (is) in darkness" (*55,5—6), *mrr.ṯn*———, *my šd.ṯn* "if ye desire———, then read!" (*21,9—22,1).

Final sentences &c.

Our conjunctions "that", "in order to", "so that", § 136.
"until" are for the most part not reproduced; the verb usually stands in the *śḏm.f* tense. Occasionally *r* (also *r-ḏd* *51,4; *r-nty.t* *30,8) introduces such sentences, Indirect interrogative sentences are introduced without a conjunction; the *nuance* of purpose and final sentences is often not perceptible. Cf. *r* with the infinitive "in order to" (§ 106); tense *śḏm.f* (§ 88).

Examples: "Remember joy, *r yy.t hrw pfꜣ n myny* till that day of death cometh" (*50,6), *dy.y mꜣ.śn* "I cause that they see" (*13,6. 10), "he said, *ꜥḥꜣ.f ḥnꜥ.y* that he (would) fight (with me)" (*42,7), "he wished, *yw.y m yry rd.wy.f* that I would be his guide (companion of his feet)" (*40,2).

Interrogative sentences.

In interrogative sentences are found the forms of the § 137.
suffix conjugation; they are usually introduced by a particle which the enclitic , *(y)r.f* (§ 69b) often follows. Such interrogative words, coming at the beginning or end of the sentence, are: *m*, accented: *yn-m*, (to *yn*: § 131) "who?", "what?"; *yḫ* "what?". General particles used to introduce

questions are: *yn yw* as first word; , *trw*, *try* as second word. Example *yn-m yn ṯw* "Who brought thee?" (*47,2.7).

Negative sentences (§ 28b).

§ 138. Principal sentences are negatived by the older particle *n* or the younger *nn* "not", which always stands first in the sentence. The verb is found in the forms of the suffix conjugation; and with the tense *śd̲m.f* after *nn* in the accented form (§ 91). *n rḫ ḥm.f* "his majesty knew not" (*51,4), *nn sp wꜥ* "not one remained" (*45,1). Likewise in the relative sentence (§ 141c).

§ 139. Dependent sentences are negatived by means of the auxiliary verbs *tm* and , *ymy* "not to be", "not to have"; the verb of which follows in the predicate (§ 98).

§ 140. Relative sentences (§ 141c) are negatived by the adjective *nyw.ty* "who is not", "who has not", which agrees in gender and number with the substantive, which it follows. It can also be used as a substantive. *nyw.ty.t* "that which does not exist" (*9,5).

Relative sentences.

§ 141. Relative sentences (cf. § 28a) are usually introduced
a by the relative pronoun , *nty*, *nty.t* "who", plural *nty.w*, which can also be used substantively. Examples: *sꜣ nty tp tꜣ* "a man who is on earth"

(*56,11), *p3 nty ḥm.f ym* "the place on which his majesty is = the palace" (*52,8), *nty.w ym.ś* "those who are in it" (*44,11), *nty.w-ym* "those who are there = the dead" (*32,4), *nty.t* "that which is (exists)" (*9,5).

The introductory "who" is often omitted in relative sentences; in which case, if the subject is the same, the verb takes the form of a participle; but if the subject is different, it prefers the relative form (§ 118): *prr.t m-b3ḥ nṯr-c3* "that which comes out before the great god (i.e. delivered as an offering)" (*19,8), "the prince, *rdy.w.n śtn* whom the king has dispatched" (*27,3), "Osiris, *nrr.w n.f nṯr.w* to whom the gods bow" (*28,9), *śḳd.w ym.ś rḫ.w.n.k* "rowers are in it (the boat) whom thou knowest (known to thee)" (*48,9). b

The relative sentence is negatived either by the negative relative *nyw.ty* (§ 140); or, in nominal sentences, by the introductory negative *n, nn* "not" (§ 138); *nn ḏrw* "there is no boundary" (*7,7), *wśḫ.t nn ḥm.ś* "a ship which has no rudder" (*43,4), "a hero, *nn śn.nw.f* who has not his like (his second)" (*42,6). c

List of Hieroglyphs.

The following list of hieroglyphics is a selection from the complete list, which Lepsius arranged according to classes for the type-foundry of Ferd. Theinhardt of Berlin. Today we know the real meaning of many signs which at that time were wrongly defined; the meaning, however, of many others is yet unknown.

After each hieroglyph there is given (in italics) the Egyptian word with which it is connected; and also how the sign is to be read, if its phonetic value is not written. Further, the classes are given (in bold-face type) in which the hieroglyphs as determinatives are placed. The list, as well as the data, is incomplete. In addition to those necessary for the reading excercises, only the most frequent hieroglyphs, phonetic values, and phrases are given.

Abbreviation: g. = god.

A. MEN

2 to call, *Cš*

5 *dwꜣ, ywꜣ,* to worship

8 *ḳꜣ, ḥꜣ*

9 to turn around, *Cny*

16 to dance, to rejoice, *kśy*

19 to bow

27 death, mummy, figure, *twt*

29 chief, officer, *wr, śmśw, śr*

30 old man, *yꜣw*

31 to smite, *ḥw*

49 *ḳwś*, to build

51 *ḳd*, to build

71 child, *ẖrd*

80 death, enemy

82 soldier, *mšC*

84 prisoner

85 enemy, foreigner

89 man, suffix § 53

91 to speak, to eat

92 sitting, weariness

98 to drink, *swr*

— to row

100 to hide, *ḥꜣp, ymn*

101 *wꜥb*, to clean

105 to carry, to work

106 *ḥḥ (n rnp.wt)*

110 the dead

117 king, suffix § 53

120 king, Osiris

121 king

128 *mynw*, *sꜣw*

128 foreigner, Bedouin

131 honourable person, *šps*

133 *ḫr*, to fall

139 honourable person, suffix § 53

B. WOMEN

3 singer, dancer

7 woman, suffix § 53

12 *yry*

15 to give birth to

16 *rnn*

C. GODS

1 *wsyr*, g. Osiris

3 *ptḥ*, g. Ptaḥ

7 g. *ṯnn* (Ptaḥ)

9 *yn-ḥr.t*, g. Onuris

10 *mnw*, g. Min

11 *ymn*, g. Amon

19 *šw*, g. Show

25 *rꜥ*, g. Re

31 *sts*, *bꜥrw* g. Set, Baal

32 *ynpw*, g. Anubis

33 *dḥwty*, g. Thot

36 *ẖnmw*, g. Khnum

54 *mꜣꜥ.t*

D. PARTS OF MAN

1 *ḏꜣḏꜣ*, *tp*

3 *ḥr*

6 hair

10 *yr*, to see (cf. *wsyr*)

12 to see

15 *ꜥyn*

17 *wḏꜣ.t*

cf. F 5

29 *r*

33 to spit, to flow out

35 *mdw*

37 back

38 *šꜥ*

39 to suckle

43 to embrace, *ḥpt*

46 *kꜣ*

47 *n*, *nyw*, negative

51 *ẖn*

52 *ꜥḥꜣ*

56 *ḏsr*

58 *ḫw*

59 *ꜥ*, for 63

62 *mḥ*, *rmn*

63 *dy, grḥ*
65 *my*
66 *ḥnk*, to distribute
69 to smite, etc., *nḫt*
76 *d*
82 *ꜣmm*
84 *ḏbʿ*
87 *dḳr*
90 *bꜣḥ*, man
90 *mt*
95 *ḥm*
96 to go, *yw, nmt, ʿḳ*
98 to go back, *pry*
99 leg, *rd*
101 *grg*
102 *ḳ*
103 *b*
110 flesh, *ḥʿ*
111 flesh

E. MAMMALS

2 horse, *ḥtr*
3 ox, *kꜣ, yḥ*
9 bound sacrificial animal
13 *yb*
14 *yw*
15 *bꜣ*
17 goat, herd, *mꜣ-ḥḏ?*
19 *śʿḥ*
22 *ẖnw*
28 baboon, rage
36 *mꜣ*
38 *rw*
49 *sꜣb, wp-wꜣ.wt*
55 *ynpw*
58 *wn*
66 bad weather, g. *śtš*

F. PARTS OF MAMMALS

3 *yḥ* instead of E 3
5 nose, to breathe, *fnḏ, šr.t, rš*
6 neck
8 *šfy.t*
15 *pḥ*
16 *ḥꜣ*
30 *ꜣ.t*
33 *wp*
35 *yꜣw.t*
41 *ʿb*
44 *ḥw, bḥ, byꜣ*
46 to hear, *śḏm, ydn*
48 *pḥ*
49 *ḫpš*
51 *whm*
58 mammals
59 *śꜣb*
60 *śt*
61 tail
63 *ywʿ, yśw*

G. BIRDS

1 *ꜣ*, also for G 5
5 *tyw*
6 *nḥ*

8 *ḥr*

13 *Ḥr Nb.ty(?)*

15 god, king

16 *ymn*

28 *ꜥẖm*

30 *mw.t*

33 *nb.ty(?)*

36 *m*

38 *m* § 13

46 *gm*

48 *ḏḥwty*

53 *byk, bꜣ*

54 *bꜣw*

58 *yꜣḫ*

60 *bnw*

66 *ḏfꜣ*

67 *sꜣ, gb* birds

71 *ꜥḳ*

73 *pꜣ*

75 *ṯnw, ḫn*

78 *ḏb*

79 *wr*

80 evil

81 *rḫy.t*

83 *w*

87 *ṯꜣ*

90 *sš*

91 *śnḏ*

92 *bꜣ*, soul

H. PARTS OF BIRDS

1 *ꜣpd*

3 *nr*

12 to fly

13 *šw, mꜣꜥ*

21 egg, goddess

I. AMPHIBIA

2 *ꜥšꜣ*

4, 7 *śbk* g. Sobk

8 *km*

9 frog, toad, *ḥḳt*

10 *ḥfn*

11 snake, goddess

16 see G 33

23 snake

26 *ḏ*

30 *f*

K. FISH

1 *yn*

2 fish

10 *ḫꜣ*

L. INSECTS

1 *byt*

3 *ḫpr*

M. PLANTS

1 tree, *ymꜣ*

9 *ḫt*

13 *rnp, ḥꜣ.t-sp*

15 *mry, try*

17 *rnp*

22 *nn, nḫb*

24 *św, śtny, (ny-śwt?)*

26 *šmꜥ*

30 *rś*

33 *y,* § 13

33 *yy (yꜣy?)* § 75

35 *śḫ.t*

36 *ꜥꜣb.t*

37 *šꜣ*

39 *ꜣḫ.t*

41 plants, *ḥn, ysy*

42 *ḥꜣ*

43 *mḥ*

47 *wꜣḏ*

63 lotos

67 *wn*

68 *ḫꜣ*

73 (late) *wḏ*

74 *ḥḏ*

77 (old) *wḏ*

80 *mś*

82 *bd.t*

89 *šnw.t*

90 vine, bower

92 fig, *dꜣb*

93 *bnr*

98 *nḏm*

N. HEAVEN, EARTH, WATER

1 heaven, *p.t, ḥry*

2 night, *kwkw*

5 *ṯḥn*

7 sun, dates, *rꜥ, hrw, śśw*

13 light, to light, *ḥnmm.t*

14 *śpd*

23 *ḫꜥ*

26 *psḏ*

28 moon, *yꜥḥ, ybd*

30 *śpr*

35 *śbꜣ, dwꜣ*

37 *tꜣ*

40 desert, foreign country, *ḫꜣś.t*

42 *dw*

44 *yꜣḫ.t*

46 district, *sp.t, ḥsp*

47 land, earth, *tꜣ, ydb* (see X 20)

48 earth, land

49 way, border, *wꜣ.t, ḥr(y)*

50 *ym* (later *m* § 13)

gś

51 stone

53 or grains

54 (sand, incense, paint)

55 *n*

mw

58 *mr*

59 pond
60 *š*
61 *šm*
66 *yw*
72 *by3*

O. BUILDINGS AND THEIR PARTS

1 city, house, *nw.t*
3 house, *pr*
6 *pr.t-r-ḫrw*
9 *h*
10 *mr, nm*
12 *ḥ.t*
17 *nb.t-ḥt* (Nephthys)
19 *Ḥ.t-ḥr*, goddess Hathor
29 *cḥc*
36 wall
43 gate, *śb3*
45 *ḳnb*
48 *ḥ3p*
51 grave, pyramid
53 *tḫn* obelisk
54 stela
61 *ḫkr*
63 *ḥb-śd*
65 feast, *ḥb*
68 steps, throne
69 door, to open, *c3*
70 *s*, bolt
71 *ys, sb, swy*
72 *ts*
74 *mnw*, g. Min
76 *ḳd*
80 *ḥ.t*, house
84 *śrḫ*

P. SHIPS AND THEIR PARTS

2 ship, *wy3*; *ḫd*, to move down stream
14 *ḫnty*, to sail up stream
16 *t3w*, *nfw*
19 *cḥc*
21 rudder
22 *ḫrw*
23 *šsp*

Q. HOUSE ARTICLES

1 *3ś* (cf. *wśyr*)
5 like 1
7 to sleep
8 to die
9 *ś*
17 *ḥtp*
19 *nś*
20 *ḫr*
25 coffin
28 *db3*
29 *ywn*
31 *ḥn*
34 *ys*

39 *mḏr*

42 dress, *mnḫ.t*

42 *mnḫ.t* + *šś* (*ˁrf?*)

51 *wḏˁ*

54 *ṯs*

58 *m3ˁ*

59 stand for images of gods and district names

R. TEMPLE ARTICLES

1 *wḏḥw*

2 *ḫ3w.t*

13 god, *nṯr*

16 *ẖry.t-nṯr*

18 *ḏd*

20 *sm3*

22 , *śn*

26 *y3b*

28 *ymy, wnm*

29 *śš3.t*

S. CLOTHING, JEWELRY, INSIGNIA

7 *ḫprš*

8 *ḥḏ*

11 *n, byty*

13 *śḫm.t*

14 *w* § 13

17 *šw.ty*

28 *yḥ*

31 *śṯ*

32 clothing

37 tongue, death, *mr, nś*

38 *ṯb.t*

39 *šn*

41 *dmḏ*

43 *ˁnḫ*

44 like 45

45 treasure, (*ḏ3s.t?*); gentilic: treasurer

48 *ˁpr*

50 *ḫrp, śḫm*

56 *ymn*

61 *ṯny*

62 *ḥḳ3*

63 *ˁw.t*

64 *w3ś, ḏˁm*

65 *w3ś.t*

66 *wśr*

75 *nḫ3ḫ3*

T. ARMS AND WAR ARTICLES

1 foreign country, *ˁ3m, ḳm3, ṯn*

2 *rś*

3 *sḫn*

9 *tpy*

10 *ḫpš*

15 to cut

20 *śšm*

21 *pd̲*

31 *śty*

33 arrow, *śḫr*, *šśr*

39 *š3*

41 *ˁ3*

43 *ḫ*

45 war-chariot

U. TOOLS AND AGRICULTURAL IMPLEMENTS

3 *śtp*

5 *nw*

8 *m3*

with Q 58 *m3ˁ*

12 *mr*, hoe

13 plough *šnˁ*

14 *tm*

19 *ty*

20 *śmn*

21 *d̲3*

24 *mr* (*3b*: U 31)

27 *mnḫ*

28 *wb3*

29 *wb3* to open

30 *ḥm*

31 *3b* (*mr*: U 24)

33 *ḫśf*

36 *nd̲*

38 *wˁ*

40 *nr.t* (Neït)

42 *šmś*

45 *mśn*, *gnw.t* *ḳrś*

48 *ś3ḫ*

49 *ḥ3p*, *ḥp*

50 *nb*

V. WICKER-WORK

1 cord, to fasten, *š3.t* 100 (cf. S 14)

2 *śt̲3*

5 *3w*

ym3ḫ

6 *šn*

6 *šś* (cf. Q 42)

8 sack, *ˁrf*

10 *ˁrḳ*

15 *mḥ*

17 *šd*

21 *ˁnd̲*

26 *w3*

27 *rwd̲*

28 *s3*

29 *s3*

30 *ḥ*

34 *śk*

37 *w3ḥ*

41 *pḫr*

43 *t̲*

44 *yt̲y*

45 *ḥśb*, to embalm (*wt*)

W. VESSELS

No.	Value
1	oil, *mrḥ.t*, *bꜣś.t*
4	*ḥs* or *ḥś*
5	water, *ḳbḥ*
6	*ḥm*
8	*ḫnt*
11	*ẖnm*
13	fluids, gifts *ḥḳt*
14	*yrṯ.t*, milk
21	*nw*, *yn*
22	*yn*
23	*yb*
23	*mꜣwṯ*
26	*wꜥb*
29	*my*
31	*wśḫ*, *ḫnw.t*
33	bread, *tꜣ*
34	*bꜣ*
35	*yt*
37	fire, cooking
39	*śnṯr*
40	*ḏr*
40	fruit
43	*nb*
46	*kꜣ*.t
49	*ḥb*, feast
53	corn, *yt*
59	copper, arms
60	*tꜣ*

X. OFFERINGS

No.	Value
3	*nḫn*
4	bread, offering
10	*pꜣw.t*
14	*sp*
19	*tꜣ*
20	*ydb* (see N 47)
22	*dy*

Y. WRITING, MUSIC AND GAME ARTICLES

No.	Value
1	*sš*
2	book, abstract
5	harp
8	*śḫm*
9	*nfr*
11	*śyꜣ*
12	*mn*

Z. STROKES AND DOUBTFUL SIGNS

No.	Value
5	*y* §13.39c.
7	*śwꜣ*, *wpy*
9	*mḏ*
10	*ḥry*
12	*t*
19	*rn*
22	*śḳr*
25	*yp.t*
30	*nm*

Vocabulary.

The vocabulary contains, besides the words necessary for the reading-exercises, other words also which are frequent in easier texts. The words are arranged according to the Egyptian alphabet (§ 12); such, however, as are written with the same hieroglyphics are placed in groups, in order that they may the more easily be found. The hieroglyphics placed before groups or single words by no means represent the whole orthography of the word in question; but are only a characteristic mark out of the orthography of the word, which is to facilitate the recognition of the word by the beginner. The numbers give the pages of the reading exercises, where the complete writing of the word can be found.

Abbreviations: g. = God. c. = country. p. = place. t. = temple.

ȝ

ȝ.t moment.

ȝwy distant, to be happy *12,8.

ȝw length *20,10. 47,10.

ȝw.t-yb joy *24,7.

ȝbw elephant, ivory.

ȝbw town Elephantine.

ȝbḫ(i?) to mix *18,7.

ȝbdw town Abydos *8,5.

ȝpd duck, goose, birds *8,8. 36,9. 45,10.

ȝmm to grasp *28,1.

ȝḥ.t field *26,7.

ȝḫ.t inundation § 48.

ȝśy to hurry, to accelerate *52,5.

ȝś.t place *9,3. 49,7.

ȝś.t goddess Isis *19,1.

ȝś.t-yb wish *19,10.

ȝś.t-ḥr inspection *24,5. 32,2.

ȝšr.t roast meat *1,9.

ȝṯp to load.

ȝṯpy.t load.

y

y oh! *21,5. § 70.

yȝw adoration, worship *31,4. 53,11.

yȝwy to be old.

yȝw.t office *15,2. 21,10.

yȝb.t the east.

ȝyb.ty east, left *55,3.

yȝr.t beans(?) *7,2.

yȝrr.t wine *25,8.

yȝḫw to be transfigured *22,9.

yȝḫw splendour *5,6.

yȝḫ excellent *14,9. 33,5.

y3ḫ.t horizon *3,7. 20,4. 55,1.
y3k.t bulblike *45,9.
yy (y3y?) to come § 75. *9,1.
yy-wy welcome! *33,9.
yʿy to wash *27,8.
yʿḥ moon *15,8.
yw to be § 122ff. § 26c. 131b.
yw(t) to come *12,8. 42,5. 51,1. § 75.
yw islsnd *13,8. 43,10. 45,2.
ywʿ to reward *26,14.
ywʿ heir, inheritance *9,7. 29,2. 33,10.
ywf meat *1,8.
ywnw town Heliopolis *11,5.
yb to believe *46,2.
yby to thirst *43,11.
yb heart *3,6. 25,7. Cf. *ḥry-yb.*
ybd month *5,1. § 48.
yp to count *34,4
yp.t-3ś.wt t. Karnak (Thebes) *4,9.
ym there *7,6. 45,8 thereof *22,8.
ym3.t goodness *12,10. 15,5.
ym3ḫ reputation *2,7.
ym3ḫy worthy, respected *2,3.4.
ymy not to be *48,7. § 139.
ymy give! *50,1. § 101.
ymy he who is in *10,1. 19,5.
ymy-yb darling *7,10.
ymy-r3 (mr) director *2,6.7.
ymn to conceal (oneself).
ymn g. Amon of Thebes *2,9.
ymn.t the west *20,1. 28,2.
ymn.ty western, right 3,7. 55,5.
yn on the part of *27,1. § 61g.
yn-m who? *47,2. § 137.
yny to bring *22,7.
ynw offering *19,3.
ynpw g. Anubis *19,4.
ynr stone *6,10. 54,6.
egg-shell *55,7.
ynḳ to enclose *52,9.
ynḥ eyebrow *46,9.
(y)nḏ-ḥr Hail! *27,10. 31,8.
yr if § 135; emphasis § 131.
With suffixes: *18,8. § 69b. § 102. § 137.
yry to make *20,3.
to create, to beget *18,7. § 115. 128.
to pass time *45,4.
auxiliary verb § 128.
yry-yḫ.t to sacrifice *11,4.
yry he who belongs to *26,6. 40,2. § 36a.
yrw figure *31,10.
yrp wine *1,8.
yrnṯ Orontes *53,8.
yrṯ.t milk *1,8.
yḥ ox *8,8. 36,9.
yḥw.ty builder, farmer.
yḫ.t affair *8,9.

yḫm.w(-śk) see *ḫm.*

ys grave *9,1. 36,5.

ysy to haste.

yśw reward *24,8.

yśṯ, yst behold, here (§ 64b) *18,1. 37,1. 51,1 ff.

it barley *7,6.

(also) *yt* (also *tf?*) father *3,2. 6,8. 10,7. 11,9. 12,2.

yt-nṯr "father of the god" (title of a priest) *49,3.

ytm g. Atum *3,7.

ytn disk of the sun *16,9. 55,2.

ytrw stream *24,1.

yṯy to take *47,4.

ydb two borders (shore?) *25,8.

ydnw representative, assistant *27,8.

C

C arm *12,9.

tp-C before *44,10. § 134.

tpy-C.wy ancestor *39,10.

m-C of *54,5.

C3 great, to be great *(C3y)*.

n-C3.t-n because *10,4.

C3b.t offering, gift.

C3m Syrian, Asiatic *13,5. 40,3.

Cyn lime-stone.

Cw.t small cattle.

Cw3y to rob.

Cb horn *38,8,

Cb3 tombstone *22,1 (cf. *ḫrp*).

Cpr to be supplied with *13,6. to fit out *56,2.

Cm to swallow.

Cny to turn around *53,10.

Cnḫ to live § 18c, the living *21,5. life *22.5.

Cnḫ ear *7,9.

Cnḏ fat.

Cry to ascend.

Crf bag (with paint?) *19,6. 36,9.

Crḳy last *18,4.

Cḥ3 to fight *37,4. 42,7.

Cḥ3 battle *13,7. arrow *42,11.

CḥC to stand *51,3. auxiliary § 127.

CḥC life-time *18,1. 55,11.

(m).CḥC.t grave *49,2.

CḥC palace *10,1. 14,6. 56,2.

Cẖm holy sparrow-hawk, idol.

Cẖnw.ty cabinet (of the king) *2,6.

Cš to call *51,5.

Cš3 to be many, many *7,4. 18,1. 37,3.
Cš3 rich *31,9.
Cḳ to go in *5,8. 23,6. 41,1.

w

w3.t way *6,2. 43,5.
w3y to bow to *(r)* *30,8.
w3w wave *45,3.
w3ḥ to lay *47,5.
w3ḥ happy, lasting *4,7.
to be happy *21,9.
w3ś happiness *4,1.
w3ś.t town Thebes *4,6.
w3śy to go to ruin *25,6.
w3ḏ green, fresh, young *16,3.
w3ḏ green paint *1,11.
w3ḏy.t goddess Uto of the Delta.
w3ḏ-wr the (Red) Sea *13,8. 44,9. 45,3.
wy how! *35,3. § 68, cf. *yy-wy.*
wy3 ship.
wC one *37,10. 40,11.
alone *55,11.
wC.ty the only one *4,10.
wCy to be alone *45,4. 53,5.
wCCw lonesomeness (of the king), palace *11,2.
wCb clean *8,9.
priest *2,1. 21,6.
wCf to fetter *6,5. 14,1.
wb3 to penetrate *27,6.
wbn to rise (sun) *12,7. 18,9. 55,3.
wp to adjust *11,3.
wpy to open *46,10.
wp-w3.wt g. Upuat *8,6. 29,8.
wn to open *6,1.
wnw.t hour *51,9.
wnn to be, to exist *36,3.
wnn-nfr Osiris *23,8. 28,3.
wnm food *55,11.
to eat *56,8.
wr great *11,1; the great one *51,2; first-born 23.8.
n-wr-n because *27,7.
wrry.t war-chariot *13,9.
wršy.t guard *43,6.
whm to repeat *4,1. 27,8.
wḥy.t stem *44,7.
wḥC to loosen.
wśyr g. Osiris *2,9. Title of the dead *9,9.
wśr to be mighty *22,9.
wśr strong *12,1. 14,5.
wśr.w might *18,2.
wśḫ far, to be wide.
wśḫ width *47,11.
wśḫ.t transport ship *43,3.
wśṯn to step out *6,4.
wšb to answer *47,8.
wt to embalm.
w.t town name? 19,5.
wtṯ to beget *49,8.

wdn to sacrifice.

wdḥw altar.

wḏ to command *29,5.
wḏ command *39,9.

wḏ3 whole, healed, to be happy *30,7. 47,5.

wḏ3 to go *56,1.

wḏ3.t holy Uzat-eye.

wḏC to judge.

wḏb shore, beach *37,3.

b

b3 to cut into pieces *54,10.
b3 to be happy(?) *18,9.
b3 soul *23,4.
b3w boat *56,2.

b3w might *13,2. 19,2. 37,8.

b3 ram, soul.

m-b3ḥ before *19,8. 46,11. out *23,10.

b3ś.ty.t goddess Bubastis (of the town *b3ś.t*).

b3ḳ olive-oil *7,4.

b3gy to be tired *33,6.

by.t honey *7,4.
byty king of Lower Egypt *4,1. 41,7.

by3 mine in Sinai *47,9.

byn bad.

byk falcon.

byk to work *16,8.
byk servant *9,11. 54,4.

bCr g. Baal *53,4.

bw place *10,2.
bw-nb each one *35,2.
bw-nfr the good § 35c.

bwt abhorrence.

bb.t whirlpool(?) *24,1.

bn.t harp *49,1.

bnw Phoenix (bird in Heliopolis).

bnw.t black granite(?) *11,10.

bnr sweet *35,3.
bnr date.

bh3 to flee *37,9,

bśy to introduce.

bšṯ to revolt *30,8.

bd.t spelt (wheat) *7,6.

bdš to become discouraged *52,6.

p

p.t heaven *6,1.

p3 to fly.
p3 to have been *54,7. § 130.
p3 this, the *41,1. § 41.
p3w.t primitive times *9,6. 16,10.
p3w.ti primitive god *8,3.

p3w.t sacrificial bread.

pC.t mankind *34,6.
pw, pwy these *28,2. § 58.
pwn.t c. Punt.
pf3 that *37,1. § 57c.
pfś see *fśy* to cook.
pnC to turn over.
pr house *2,8.
pr-ḥd treasury *3,10.
pr-C3 pharaoh *56,1.
pr.t winter *8,4. 18,4. § 48.
pry to ascend, to come out *6,3. 23.6. 40,11.
to be delivered up *19,8.
pr.t-r-ḫrw sacrifice for the dead *8,8.
pry hero *42,6.
prsn baking *1,9.
pḥ to get *43,9.
pḥ.t strength.
pḫr to draw through *33,7.
pśḏ back *13,11. 19,3.
pśḏ.t the ninefold gods (family of) *32,3.8.
ptn desert between Egypt and Syria *43,9.
ptr behold! *59,1.
pḏ.t bow *16,2.

f

f3y to carry.
fnḏ nose *43,1. 49,10. 50,1.
fḫ to loose.
fśy (later *pśy*) to cook *44,6.
fḳ3 to reward.

m

m preposition § 61a.
m-m together with *23,8.
m3 (m3y?) lion *30,9.
m3-ḥs lion *53,9.
m33 to see *12,5. 23,5. 43,6.
m3C true *33,11. genuine *46,9.
m3C-ḫrw to justify *29,3.
blessed *2,1—5.
triumph *18,2.
m3C.t right *11,3. 32,9.
m3wṯ red granite *12,3.
m3ḥ garland *50,2.
m3-ḥḏ Oryx-Antilope *4,4.
my how *4,3. then *22,1. § 135.
my.ty the like *16,10. 54,7.
r-my.ty.t in like manner *26,6.
mynw herdsman.
myny to land, to die; see *mn.*
mw water *1,10. 44,5.
mw.t mother *16,1.
mw.t goddess Mut of Thebes.
mwt to die *44,1.
mn to remain, to last *10,5,
mn-yb brave *33,9.
myny to land, to die *39,10. 50,7.
mnC.t wet-nurse *19,11.
mnw monument *6,8.
mnw g. Min *29,11.

mnw.t dove *19,7.
mnfy.t army, staff *31,3.
mnmn to tremble *46,3.
mnmn.t herd *7,7. 42,9.
mnḫ to be excellent *14,5.
mnḫ excellent *20,6.
mnḫ.t dress *1,11.
mntw g. Mont *43,2. *53,3.
mr s. *ymy-r3* director.
mr to be sick.
mr pyramid.
mry to love *10,4. 16,2.
mrw.t love *14,8.
or *n-mrw.t* (§ 62b) therewith *10,5.
out of love for *12,7.
mr.t subordinates, slaves *14,10.
mrḥ.t oil *1,11.
mḥ to fill *5,6.
to be full *20,11.
mḥ-yb darling *3,11.
mḥ.t the north (Delta) *7,11.
mḥ.ty northern *17,11. 40,1.
mḥy.t north-wind *23,11.
mḥ ell *6,9. 20,9. 46,6.
ms to bring.
mśy to give birth to *15,7.
mśw.t birth *4,1.
mśn.ty stone-cutter *2,3.
m.śdm.t black paint *1,11.
mśḏy to hate *36,4.

mšʿ army *2,6. 30,11.
mšw dagger *41,3.
mky to protect *14,1.
mk.t protection *33,2.
mt see *mwt* to die.
mty director(?) *21,7.
mtn chief *44,3.
md.t speech *51,6.
mdw to speak *55,7.
mḏr to press.
mḏr-w3.t to be true *41,10.

n

n preposition § 61c. genetive § 21c.
n (nyw?) not 51,4. 54,7. § 138.
nyw.ty he who is (has) not *33,6. § 140.
nyw.tyt that which does not exist *9,5.
nn not *26,9. 42,6. 43,4. 45,1. § 138.
nyś to call.
nw.t (nnw.t?) goddess of heaven Nut *28,7.
nw.t town, residence *2,7.
nw.ty municipal *21,11.
nwy flood *34,9.
nb each, every, all anyone *4,9. 13,2. 19,2. 21,8. § 37b.
nb master *2,7. 9,11. 40,1.
nb.t mistress *2,8. 20,1.

nb.ty (?) "the two goddesses of the land," title of a king *4,7.

nb.t-ḥ.t goddess Nephthys.

nb gold *3,10. 26,4.
nb.t town Nubt.
nb.ty g. Nubti (Set); cf. *Ḥr.*

nbś Sycomore (?) *1,10.

nfw aspiration, breath *22,5. (cf. *ṯ3w*).

nfr beautiful, good *18,1.
nfrw beauty *16,1. 55,4.
nfr.t girl *56,2.
nfry.t-r until *18,4. § 62c.

nmt to wander *40,1.

nn this *10,3. 44,1. § 57e.

nrw strength *6,6.
nr.t mankind *34,6.

nr.t goddess Neit of Sais.

nrr to bow (?) *28,9.

nh.t Sycomore.

nhrn Naharina (Mesopotamia) נהרים *17,11. 37,1. 40,4.

nḥb.t nape of the neck *42,11.

nḥm to take away.

nḥḥ eternity *6,4; only written *31,8.

nḥśy negro, Nubian *38,11.

nḫ3ḫ3 whip.

nḫb town Elkab.
nḫb.t goddess Nechbet.

nḫn (cf. *s3w*) town Nechen *4,4. 54,1.

nḫn to be a child *10,2.

nḫt to be strong, strong *4,6.
nḫt strength, victory *13,1. 14,2. 40,6.

nś tongue.
nś belonging to, according to measure *46,6.

nś.t throne 18,11.
nś.t-t3.wy t. Karnak *6,8.

nty which § 141a.
nty.t the existent *9,5.
nty.w-ym the dead *32,4.
r-nty.t that *30,8. § 136.

nṯr god *8,2.
nṯry to be divine *16,4.
nṯry divinity (?) *31,5.
nṯr-nfr good god: king *20,1.
Cf. *ḥ.t-nṯr*, *ḥm-nṯr*, *ḫry.t-nṯr*.

nḏ(y) to deliver, to protect *33,5.
nḏ(.ty) deliverer *12,6. 13,10.

nḏm sweet, pleasant *12,10. 22,5.

ndś small *47,2.

r

r preposition § 61b; after imperative *38,4. § 102; with infinitive § 106.
conjunction: § 136; cf. *yr.*

r3 mouth *7,9. 36,8.
saying *56,9.
r3 goose *19,7.
r3-pr temple *12,8.
r3-3w p. Tura (quarry) *54,6.

r3-ḥry supreme director *39,7.
r3-śṯ3.w p. Sakkara *23,6.
ymy-r3 (mr) director *2,6. 39,8.
rC g. Re *6,3. 4,3.
rwḏ to thrive *10,6.
rwḏ feast *24,8.
rwd steps *9,4.
rpC.ty (yry-pC.t?) prince *3,7.
yry.t-pC.t(?) princess *15,5.
r.f *18,8; cf. *yr*.
rm fish *45,10.
rmny to carry.
rmṯ man *3,6. 26,2.
rn name *7,1. 10,5.
rnpy fresh, to be young.
rnpy.t flowers, fruit *15,2.
rnp.t Calendar-(year) *5,10. 14,2.
rnn to bring up *16,2. 25,9. 38,5—7.
rḫ to know, to be acquainted with *26,3. 48,9. 51,4. § 82.
rḫy.t mankind *31,2.
rś south (Upper Egypt).
rśy southern *8,10. 17,10. 40,1.
ryś to awake.
ršw.t joy *50,6.
ršrš to be glad *31,3.
rk time *49,6.
r.k *38,4; cf. *r*.
rṯnw Syria *13,5. 42,5.

rd leg *40,2. (dual *rd.wi*).
rdy to give § 74.
rdy to give § 74.
to appoint *54,3.

h

h3 o! § 70.
h3y to descend *30,2. 47,9.
h3b to send *27,6.
hy to rejoice *31,3.
hy husband.
hp law *17,2.
hmhm.t roaring *13,9.
hny to bow.
hnw to shout with joy *31,2.
hry to be satisfied.
hrw day *27,11. 43,7.
hdhd to attack *37,6.

ḥ

ḥ.t house, fortress *43,6.
ḥ.t-nṯr temple *2,11. § 18a.
ḥ.t-ḥr goddess Hathor *2,8.
ḥ3.ty heart *34,11.
ḥ3.ty the first one § 47.
ḥr ḥ3.t before *37,11. 52,7. 54,8.
ḥ3.t-sp year of reign. § 48a.
ḥ3.ty-C count *2,3.
§ 38.
ḥ3 behind *51,3.
ḥ3y.t mourning *33,7.

ḥꜣw naked *30,5.
ḥ(ꜣ)p to conceal.
ḥ(ꜣ)pw.ty spy *51,7. 10.
ḥꜣ-nb.w Greeks etc. *34.7.
ḥꜣḳ to rob *42,9.
ḥyḥy to seek *33,6.
ḥʿ limb, body *12,9. 18,7.
ḥʿy to rejoice *12,5.
ḥʿpy Nile *22,7.
ḥwy to smite *42,8.
ḥb feast *28,10.
ḥb-śd reign-jubilee *15,11.
ḥbś to clothe.
ḥbś dress *30,5.
ḥpy Apis, bull in Memphis.
ḥpt to embrace.
ḥfꜣw snake, dragon *46,5.
ḥfn 100000. § 46.
ḥm.t wife *3,2. 15,5. 17,9.
ḥmw rudder *43,4.
ḥmśy to sit *38,3.
ḥm majesty *5,1.
ḥm servant, slave *26,6.
ḥm-nṯr prophet *2,9. § 18a.
ḥm-kꜣ priest of the dead *21,6.
ḥm.t female slave *26,6.
ḥmw.t handicraft, art *2,11.
ḥmw.ty workman *2,2. 20,3.8.
ḥmt copper *41,3.
ḥnʿ together with *6,3. 37,2. 7,2.

ḥnw.t mistress.
ḥnmm.t mankind *34,6.
ḥnk to present.
ḥnk.t offering *23,2.
ḥr g. Horus *19,1; title of a king *4,1.
Ḥr Nb.ty(?) "Horus, (conqueror of) Nubti [= Set]": title of a king *4,7.
ḥr sight, face.
ḥr-nb each one *35,1.
ḥr preposition § 61d.
m-ḥr-n before, on *52,4.
ḫft-ḥr in the presence of *26,5.
r-ḫft-ḥr in the presence of *50,5.
ḥry the supreme *2,11. 14,10. 39,8.
ḥry.t desert *3,8.
ḥry-yb dwelling in *8,6.
ḥry-ḏꜣḏꜣ chief *4,4. 8,2. 29,11.
ḥry to withdraw *51,3.
ḥry.t terror *13,3. 39.1.
ḥḥ cf. *ḥyḥy* to seek, *nḥḥ* eternity.
ḥḥ million.
ḥḥ n rnp.wt million years *15,11. 27,4.
ḥsy to praise *19,10. 21,1.
ḥsw.t favour, love *15,5. 20,1. 26,3.
ḥśy to sing *50,5.
ḥsy singer *49,1.
ḥsꜣ see *mꜣ* lion.
ḥśb to calculate *9,9. 15,1. 55,11.

ḥḳ.t beer *1,8. 8,8.

ḥḳ.t goddess Hekt (toad) *29,8.

ḥḳꜣ to rule *16,2.

ḥḳꜣ ruler *9,8. 15,7.

ḥḳꜣ.t rule *34,2.

ḥḳr hungry *3,5. 30,4.

ḥknw praise *43,2.

ḥtp to sit down, to rest *19,1. 55,5.
to set (sun) *3,7.

ḥtp peace *9,1. 24,7. 54,9.

ḥtp.t food *19.7.

ḥtm to go to ruin *26,9.

ḥtr team (of horses) *37,2. 52,2.

nt-ḥtr charioteer *52,6.

ḥḏ to become bright *18,8. 43,9.

ḥḏ, white, silver.

ḥḏ.t crown of Upper Egypt *34,3.

ḫ

ḫ.t see *yḫ.t* affair.

ḫ.t tree cf. *ḫt.*

ḫꜣ thousand *19,6.

ḫꜣy.t slaughter *40,8.

ḫꜣw night *43,8.

ḫꜣw.t altar *23,10.

ḫꜣrw Syria *55,9.

ḫꜣś.t desert, foreign country *14,1. 51,2.

ḫꜣś.ty foreigner, Bedouin *31,1.

ḫCy to appear, to shine *55,1.
glittering *4,6. 6,7.

ḫCw brightness, crowns *4,7.

ḫC.w arms *13,7.

ḫCr to rage *53,2.

ḫwy to protect.

ḫbśw.t beard *46,7.

ḫpy to die *36,4.

ḫpr to become, to happen *18,9.

ḫpr form, appearance *11,7. 23,3.

ḫpš power *17,3.

ḫft until, on *20,3. according to *36,2.

ḫft-ḥr, r-ḫft-ḥr cf. *ḥr.*

ḫfty enemy.

ḫm not to know *39,1.

yḫm.w-śk the star which does not set (circumpolar) *31,2.

ḫmt three.

ḫmt to think *42,8.

ḫny to flutter, to lie down *43,10.

ḫnt forehead *38,9.

ḫnt before *39,2.

ḫnty the foremost, the first.

ḫnty imn.tyw god of the dead of Abydos *8,7.

ḫnty to go up stream, to journey southward *56,5.

ḫr with, preposition § 61f; but *51,9. § 64b.

ḫr to fall *43,1.11.
ḫr hostile prince *37,1. 51,1.
ḫrw voice *46,1.
ḫrw enemy *33,3. army *52,9.
ḫrp to lead *27,4; to advance *53,5.
ḫrp leader, director *3,9.
ḫrp stela, tomstone *22,1 (cf. Cbꜣ).
ḫśbḏ lapislasuli *46,9.
ḫśf to keep off.
ḫśfyw to draw near *32,5.
ḫ.t tree *7,5. 46,3.
ḫt-n-Cnḫ tree of life *34,10.
ḫt in *32,9.
m-ḫt afterwards *30,10. future *50,11.
ḫtf written instead of ḫft.
ḫtm seal, to seal.
ḫtꜣ Hittite *51,1.
ḫdy to go down stream, to journey northward *43,5. 52,8. 56,5.

h

h.t body *28,7. belly *46,11.
hꜣb.t "wire" of the crown *38,9.
hny to row *56,4.
hny.t sailor *26,1.
hnw the inside, palace *48,8. 56,2.
m-hnw in *41,1. 55,8.
hnm to unite with *12,9.
hnmw g. Chnum *29,8.

hr under *39,9. § 61e.
hry he who carries, possessor *55,11.
hry.t necessity of life *34,4.
hry.t-nṯr graveyard, underworld *6,2. 56,8.
hry-ḥb reading priest.
hrd child *21,10.
hsy miserable *30,8. 37,1.
hkr jewelry, arms *13,6.

s

s(ꜣ?) man *40,3. 55,10.
sꜣ son *2,7. sꜣ.t daughter *3,1.
sꜣ protection *12,9. 3,4.
sꜣ Phyle (priest's staff) *21,7.
sꜣw watchman.
sꜣw Nḫn title of an official *54,1.
sꜣb judge *54,3.
swy(?) to go.
sby to pass away *49,6.
swr (later swy) to drink *24,1.
sp time *26,4. 47,2. property *31,5. misfortune *33,4. example *31,5. 37,6.
sp ever *16,10. 54,7.
spy to remain over *45,1.
spꜣ.t district *30,2.
smꜣy to unite *38,4.
smy.t cemetery.

sny to pass by.
snw bread *23,9.
sḫn.t support of heaven *13,3.
ssm cf. *śśm* horse.
sš writer *14,11.
to write *35,10.
sš swamp *56,6.
sšn blossom of the lotus *50,2.
skr g. of the dead in Memphis.

ś

śꜣ back.
m-śꜣ behind *41,2. 53,9.
śꜣy to become satisfied.
śꜣḥ to present with *26,7.
to get *44,10.
śyꜣ to perceive, to recognise *44,3.
ś.yꜣḫ to glorify *28,6.
ś.Cꜣy to enlarge *39,6.
ś.Cnḫ to animate.
śCḥ nobility, dignity *5,5. 28,3.
knight *39,5.
ś.CḥC to set up, to reach *6,9. 16,6.
św3y to pass by *21,8. 36,5.
ś.wꜣš to praise *31,5.
śwḥ.t egg *55,7.
świ but § 64c.
ś.wḏ to order *21,10.
śbꜣ star.
śbꜣ door, gate *6,9. 16,6.
śbḥ to cry 43,1.
śp.t lip, coast.
śpr to get *40,4.
śpdd to make ready, to be § 77.
ś.fḫy to loosen.
śmꜣ to kill.
śmꜣ sacrificial bull *13,11.
ś.mꜣC to justify *35,9.
ś.mꜣC-ḫrw to justify *56,10.
ś.mꜣwy to renew.
śmy to announce.
ś.mn to establish *15,10. 17,2.
ś.mnḫ to embellish, to mend *10,9. to do good *41,10.
śmr friend (royal title) *2,1.
śmśw the elder *9,6. 32,8.
śn brother *3,3. 32,7.
śn.t sister, wife *19,10. 50,2.
śn.nw the second, companion *42,6. 45,5.
śn to smell, to kiss.
śn-tꜣ to worship *32,4.
śnb to be well *2,1. health *24,7.
ś.nfr to embellish *14,6.
ś.nḫn to bring up (child) *5,5.
śnṯr incense *1,10. 22,4.
śnḏ to be afraid *48,7.
śnḏ fear *13,2. 43,6.

ś.nḏm to sit *47,4. 50,4.

śnḏr c. Sendar *40,7.

śr officer *21,8. prince *40,11.

śrḫ throne *19,1.

śḫw to assemble *37,1.

ś.ḥmy to drive back *33,4.

ś.ḥry to withdraw *18,6.
to drive away *33,3.

ś.ḥtp to rejoice *30,6.

ś.ḥḏ to clear up *16,9. 55,4.

śḫ.t field.

śḫꜣ to think of *50,6.
śḫꜣw remembrance *32,6.

śḫm to have power over (*m*) *23,3. 37,7. 38,5.
śḫm mighty *9,7.
śḫm-t might *35,4.
śḫm.t double crown *38,7.

śḫm Sistrum (women's rattle).

śḫr kind *55,6. plan, advice.

ś.ḫr to cast down *31,1.

śḫśḫ to run *41,1.

śḫr to cover *46,8.

ś.śꜣy to satisfy *45,11.

śśw day of the month *5,1. § 48a.

śśm, ssm horse *26,11.
ssm.t mare *40,11.

ś.śn to breathe *22,5.

śšꜣ.t Seschat, goddess of writing.

śšm to lead *20,3.

śḳr (later *śḳy*) to smite *13.5.
śḳr-Cnḫ prisoner *26,11.

ś.ḳd rower *48,1.

śk to pass (away) cf. *yḫmn.w-śḳ*.

ś.gr to silence *50,8.

ś.grḥ to appease *17,2.

śty to throw, to close *42,10.
śty Bedouin *44,2.
śtw.t light rays *20,11.

śtny (ny-św.t?) king of Upper Egypt *3,8. 4,1.11. 5,10.
śtny.t kingdom *4,7. 29,5.

śṯ see, as *25,5. § 64b.

śṯꜣ winding.

śṯy.t Syria *13,4.
śṯ.ty Syrian *17,3.

śṯp to choose.
śṯp chosen *14,3. 48,2.

śd tail *41,5.

śdꜣdꜣ to tremble § 77.

śḏm to hear *30,10. 46,1.

š

š pond *8,10. 56,1.

šꜣw destiny *49,5.
šꜣC to begin.
šꜣC-m begun from *18,3.

šC sand *37,3. 52,2.

ḥry-šC Bedwin *54,10.
šC.t cake *1,9.
šCd to cut *41,5.
šw feather.
šw g. Schow.
šw.ty double feather (as a king's crown) *38,10.
špśy, *špśś* to be venerable.
špśy venerable *2,10. 12,11.
špś stela *21,8.
šfy.t appearance, might *3,6. 16,7.
šmy to go *43,8. 44,7. 48,10.
šmw summer *5,1.
šmC to play, to dance *50,5.
šmCy.t dancer *2,5.
šmC Upper Egypt *54,1.
šmśy to follow, to serve *9,10. 40,1. 50,10.
šmśw servant *2,2. 52,10.
šny to surround *24,5.
šny hold back from *(m)* *23,7.
šnC granary.
šnw.t shed *3,9.
šnb.t skin, body *12,10. 50,2.
šr.t nose.
šsp to receive, to take *13,7. 23,9. to conceive *49,9.
šś linen *8,8.
šś corn *15,1.
šśr arrow.
št3 secret *31,10.
šdy to suckle *5,7. 20,2.
šdy to read *22,1.
šdy.t town Crocodilopolis (in the Fayoum province) 4,3.

ḳ

ḳ3y to be high.
ḳ3 height *20,9.
ḳ3b to double.
ḳbb cool, to be glad *56,3. 56,7.
ḳbḥw cool water *1,10.
ḳm3 to create, to do *16,1.
ḳmy anointing-oil *50,1.
ḳny to be strong.
ḳny brave *15,7. 26,8.
ḳny.t strength *13,1. *18,2.
ḳnb.t officials.
ḳnd to be angry.
ḳry thunder *46,1.
ḳrśw coffin *54,6.
ḳrś.t burial *20,1.
ḳd to build.
ḳd character.
ḳdšw town Cadesh *40,10. 51,3.

k

k3y to think *42,9.
k3 Ka (guardian spirit, genius, etc.).
k3 bull *4,6. 28,1.
k3.t work *4,9. 20,3.
k3.t wife *49,9.
k3ry Nubian country *17,10.

k3p to smoke.
k(3)š (fem.!) c. Nubia כוש *27,6.
kyy, *ky.ty* the, the other § 43.
kwkw darkness *55,6.
kf3 to unveil *46,4.
km to complete *18,1.
km.t Egypt *14,1. 44,4.
km-wr Isthmus of Suez *43,10.
kśy to bow *19,2.
kš see *k3š*.

g

gbb g. Geb *28,6.
gbgb to cast down *37,10. 53,7.
gmy to find *25,5. 45,8. 46,5.
gmḥ to perceive *44,2. 53,1.
gmḥ.t crown *38,10.
gmgm to crack(?) *46,3.
gnw.t chronicles *15,10.
gr to be silent.
gr.t but *56,9. § 64c.
grḥ rest, night.
grg to lay a trap *51,3.
gś side *11,3. 50,4.
r-gś near *52,11.

t

t3 bread *1,9. 15,1.
t3 earth, land.
t3-mry Egypt *34,7.
t3-śty Nubia *52,2.
t3-ḏśr cemetery *8,6. 19,5.
t3š border *17,10.
tyty to tread under foot *13,4.
twt figure, form.
twt to unite *50,1 ("altogether").
tp head. *tp-ˁ* see *ˁ*.
tp upper part, terrace *20,5.
tp upon, on *23,5.
tpy he who is upon *19,5. 21,5.
tpy.t best oil *50,1.
tpy-ˁ.wy forefather, ancestor *39,10.
tpy the first *5,3. 32,7. § 47.
tpy to breathe *49,10.
tf see *yt* father.
tm not to be *11,3. 56,8. § 98. § 139.
try time *43,8.
tḫn obelisk *16,6. 20,8.

ṯ

ṯ3y man *49,8.
chicken *55,7.
ṯ3.ty vizier *2,7. 52,4.
ṯ3w wind (cf. *nfw*).
ṯw thou, thee *5,5 ff.
ṯb.t sandal, sole.
ṯpḥ.t cave *22.7.

ṯny to lift.

ṯny town This, Thinis district *9,2. 27,5.
ṯntꜣ.t throne *38,3.
ṯḥwḥw to rejoice *35,1.
ṯḥn to collide *37,5.

ṯḥn to shine.

ṯs knot, to tie.

ṯsy to lift *29,4.

d

d.t hand.
dꜣb fig *1,9. 7,2. 45,8.

dy to give § 74.
to appoint *41,11.
dy-Cnḫ to give life § 128a.
m-dy together with, of *51,10.

dwꜣ to adore *27,1. 32,1.
dwꜣ to become morning *18,8.
dwꜣy.t morning *23,5.
dwn to stretch out, to move *45,6.
dbḥ to request *54,5.
dp.t ship *44,11.

dp.t taste *44,1.

dmḏ to unite.
("united") *32,5.
dr to drive away.
drp to sacrifice *23,8. 36,7.
dšr red.

dḳr fruit *7,5.
ddwn Nubian g. *25.2.

ḏ

ḏ.t eternity, eternal *4,3. 6,11.

ḏꜣy to cross over *43,3.
ḏꜣmw generation *49,7.
ḏꜣḏꜣ.t college *21,7. 35,11.

ḏꜣḏꜣ head *13,5.
ḥry-ḏꜣḏꜣ being upon.
chief *4,4. 8,2. 10,10.
ḏC storm *44,9. 48,3.

ḏCm elektron (silver-gold) *16,8. 20,5.10.

ḏw mountain *19,5.
ḏw (ḥw?) bad.

ḏb.t brick *25,5.

ḏbꜣ to replace.

ḏbC seal, to seal.
ḏfꜣ food *19,7.

ḏrw border *7,7.
ḏr since *16,10. 39,10. § 134.
r-ḏr whole *26,5. (§ 44).

ḏḥwty g. Thot *35,10.
ḏś self § 44a.

ḏśr splendid *4,7. 31,9.
ḏd to say *9,9. 21,2.
r-ḏd that *51,4.11.

ḏd to last, to exist.
ḏd.t duration *24,7.
ḏdw town Busiris *8,5. 29,7.

Remarks on the Reading Exercises.

The reading exercises are easier texts gathered in such a way that out of the simpler sentences of the texts a connected paragraph was chosen or formulated. More difficult parts of the text are completely dispensed with. Nowhere is anything added; only in a few cases an exceptional orthography had to be replaced by the customary one of the same word. The separation of words and the placing of signs have been carried out in such a way that the beginner can easily recognize the separate word-pictures; in this respect the antique originals look different, but this had to be withheld from the beginner.

The reading exercises are to be taken in order, and, in fact, only after the sections referred to in the margin have been studied. The difficulty of the texts grows gradually, although the simple language and the clear unity of words of the classical age predominate. It is only at the end that examples of the freer vernacular of the New Kingdom and the antique of the Old Kingdom are given. The contents are quite dissimilar. Single words and short titles form the beginning. Besides the temple inscriptions of kings, there are inscriptions from the graves of men in private life; then there are hymns to gods, and finally some belles-lettres.

In the following remarks the numbers *1—*56 with the number of the line refer to the reading exercises. The section marks (§§) refer to the grammar, and the designations O3, M74 to the list of hieroglyphs (page 54 ff.). Egyptian words in italics are found in the vocabulary (page 63 ff.). With the assistance of the helps already mentioned the hieroglyphics are to be transcribed into Latin letters according to § 19, and a complete written translation should be made. Then try to re-translate into hieroglyphics the transcription as well as the translation without helps.

Page ***1**, 2—7: Alphabet (§ 12), together with the latin transcription, should be copied often until complete ease is acquired. In like manner all printed groups are shortened.

***1**, 8—11: for reading, writing, and translating: single words out of lists of offerings. ***2,** 1—3: names of men, preceded by a title and followed by *m3C-ḫrw* "blessed" in different forms. Proper names with a meaning should always be analysed into their component parts and translated. ***2,** 4—5: names of women, as in 1—3. ***2,** 6—11: names of men and women with titles and epithets. ***3,** 1—2: names of family relations followed by proper names. ***3,** 3—4: two men with statement of relationship or titles. ***3,** 5—7: sentences with verbal forms; 8—11: titles of two officials. 9: § 39. 9: Inny. 10: *pr-ḥḏ* O3 + M74; § 39. ***4:** titles, 1—3 and 6—8 of two kings (Amenemhet I. and Thutmose III.), 4—5 and 9—11 of three officials. 1: *dy-Cnh* presented with life. 4: district of the Oryx-Antilope (N 46, Q 59, E 17). ***5,** 1—2: date from Abydos, during the time of king Amenhotep I. 2: *mry* beloved. ***5,** 3: title of a priest and of a temple-official. ***5,**4-8: address of the goddess Hathor to king Thutmose III. The suffix *y* "my" is not written, or is represented by the woman (§ 53). 7: "milk" is plural § 37 b. ***5,** 9—11: address of a god to the king. 9: *dy.n.y.* 11: § 133. ***6,** 1—4: hymn to the dead. Order of words § 55. ***6,** 5—11: dedicatory inscription on a lime-stone door in the Amon-temple of Amenhotep I. at Karnak. 6—7: title of a king. 8,11: § 133. ***7,** 1—7: description of a fertile land in Syria; the verb "to be" is usually not expressed (§ 27). 1: § 58. 2: § 61 a. 3: § 55. 7: § 138. ***7,** 8—11: high-priest of Amon. 10: *ntr-nfr* the king. *** 8,** 1—3: Amon of Karnak and Luxor. ***8,** 4—11: dated sacrificial formula ("day one") for Antef; *ḥtp dy śtn* "an offering which the king gives", is a shortened formula for "offering". 6—7: § 63. 8: § 88. ***9,** 1—9: the dead speaks from the grave. 2: *yry.n.y* "I have built (it)"; first the district *t3-wr* "Thinis", then the town *3bḏw* "Abydos" which is in it. 4—8: epithets of Osiris. 5: § 140, 141. 8: *nty.w* "the existing". ***9,** 9—10; 2: *śš* relates personal experiences. 1: dweller in the palace = king. ***10,** 3—8: Thutmose I. relates why and for what purpose he restored the temple of Osiris in Abydos. 3: *ḥm.y* "my majesty". 4,5: § 64. 4: § 92. ***10,** 9—11: chief builder and high-priest of Amon. 9: § 106. ***11,** 1—3: address of a vizier, chief-justice. 3: § 98. ***11,** 4—11: dedication on a granite door in the Amon-temple of Thutmose III. at Heliopolis.

10: § 109. 11: § 128. §**12,** 1—4: dedication on a granite door in the Amon-temple of queen Hatshepsut; the words and suffixes relating to it have feminine forms only in part. 3: § 109; *ḏśr mnw ymn* is the name of the door. 4: § 128b. ***12,** 5—13; 11: "poetical stela", Amon addresses Thutmose III. 12,5: § 82, 105. 7: § 62. 8: § 105. 9: § 39a. 10: § 68. ***13,** 1: § 105. 4,8: *yy.n.y* is almost without meaning; *tyty.k*: § 88; *ymy.w*: § 63. 5: *śḳr* § 30. 6: § 88; *Cpr*: § 82. 11: § 82. ***14,** 1—7: titles of Rameses II. and Psamtik I.; the epithets begin with an adjective or participle. 1: *mk* according to § 13. ***14,** 8—11: royal official. 9: lord of the palace = the king. ***15,** 1—3: recorder of bread and corn. ***15,** 4: note about a woman who sits beside her husband.

***15,** 5—6: Hatshepsut, wife of the king. ***15,** 7—8: address of a king. 7: read *mry RC* 7, 8: § 115. ***15,** 9—11: address of Thoth to Thutmose III., whose title he establishes. 9: *yry.y* "I make". 10: *śmn.y*. 11: *yry* participle. ***16,** 1—2: address of Hathor to the king. 1: *ḳmꜣ.t* participle. 2: *rnn.y* "I brought up"; *my*: § 64; *mrr.y*: § 92; *ḥkꜣ*: § 106; the "nine-bow (people)" are the arch-enemies of the Egyptians. ***16,** 3—11: dedication for the two obelisks of Hatshepsut in Karnak. 6: § 109. 7: name of door. 10: § 96. 11: § 133. ***17,** 1—11: scarab of Amenophis III. in commemoration of his marriage with *Tyy* whose parents were of simple birth. ***18,** 1—19, 3: death of Thutmose III. and accession of Amenophis II. 1: § 64b. 3: *šꜣC-m* "of". 4: *nfry.t-r* "until". 7: *ḥC.w nṯr* of the body of the king; *yry*: § 113. 8: § 69b.

***19,** 2: later sign for *m* § 13. ***19,** 4—9: sacrificial formula from the grave of *Nḫty*; Anubis is to give thousands of offerings to the dead. 5: epithets of Anubis. 8: § 112. ***19,** 10—20. 2: note on a woman, who was the wet-nurse of the king. 10: *śn.t.f* for "his wife", namely of the lord of the grave; *n-ꜣś.t-yb.f* "his darling". 11: *Ḥr* the king. ***20,** 3—11: two verses from the strophically arranged autobiography of a chief of builders. 3: *ḥmw.tyw* "hand artist". 4: *ḥ.t-nṯr* "temple" with two further poetical descriptions of the same. ***21,** 1—4: acclamation to the visitor of a grave, who should pray for the buried person. 1: *mrr*: § 113; *ḥss*: § 92. 2: § 116. 4: § 115. ***21,** 5—22, 11: detailed appeal of the same kind. 5: § 70. 8: § 116. 9: § 135. 11:

nw.tyw "the town-gods" i. e. the gods of the mother city. ***22,** 1: *my* "so". 4: § 88. 5: § 104. 6: § 120. 9, 10: § 104. ***23,** 1—**24,** 3: offering formula with wishes for the life of the dead in the future. 3 ff.: infinitive, dependent on *dy.f.* 6: *Cḳ pr.t* "to go in and out again". 7: § 96. 8: § 95; *m-m* "together with". 10: § 113. **24,** 1: *swr* § 30. ***24,** 4—8: Amon speaks to Hatshepsut. 5: § 120. 6: *mrr.y*; *ṯn*: § 50. 8: *yry.w.n.ṯ n.y* § 120. ***24,** 9—11: address of Amon to Thutmose III. 9: *s3.y.* 11: § 128. ***25,** 1—11: dedication of the Dedwen-temple of Thutmose III. at the second cataract. 3: king Sesostris III. made a god. 4: § 109; Nubian sand-stone. 5: 64 b; it fails him. 6: § 66 a. 7: "as something which a son did" § 118. 8—9: epithets of "father" § 112. 10: order of words § 55: Thutmose speaks in the first person. ***26,** 1—11: Admiral Ahmose relates his deeds. 3: *ḫpr.t* § 114. 4: § 82. 5: *ḏr.f* § 44. 6: § 66 b. *yry.w* "those who belong thereto". 7: § 66 a. 8—9: proverb. 8. *ynyry.t.n.f* § 120. ***27,** 1—**29,** 4: Osiris hymn. ***27,** 1—8: title of the suppliant, usually introduced by relative forms § 118. 1: *yn* § 61 g, 107. 2. *śmnḫ* § 106. 4: read *n ḥḥ n rnp.wt* "of millions of years". 5: *t3-wr* "district of Abydos". 7: *ḥr-yb* of the king § 133. 10: § 70. ***28,** 1—**29,** 1: epithets of Osiris. 1—4: play on the words *k3* and *nfr*. 2: *pwy* for *pw* § 57 b. 6: *śy3ḫ* "who glorifies him". 9 ff. active relative form § 118, between which are passive participles § 112; both with *n.f* "for him", "to him". 11: is it *yry.w.n* § 118 "which was made for him" or is *mk.t.f* omitted as *33, 2? ***29,** 2: Geb, father of Osiris. 4: appeal to Osiris, § 99. ***29,** 5—6: address of the god-king. 5: *wḏ.n.y s3.y n ḫ.t.y.* ***29,** 7—**30,** 6: offering formula for Antef, who finally speaks himself. 11: district-prince of the Min-district (Panopolis, Achmim). ***30,** 2—6: first person singular. 3: § 120. 6: § 120. ***30,** 7—**31,** 5: Nubian war of Thutmose II. 7: § 87; "to rejoice the heart of his majesty" = to announce to him. 9: § 90. 8, 10: § 64 a. 11—1: § 124 b. ***31,** 2—3: § 132. ***31,** 6—**33,** 7: Osiris hymn, consisting only of epithets. ***32,** 1: passive participle. 2: the circumpolar stars. 4: "those tarrying there" = the dead. 5: *ḫśf.w* § 106. 11 ff.: § 118. ***33,** 2: Isis; *mk.t* § 13. 3—7: epithets of Isis. 6: *b3gy.* ***33,** 8—**36,** 2: the appointment of Horus as world-

ruler; from a hymn to Osiris, who is addressed in **35**, 7. ***33**, 8: *ršrš*. 9: § 68. 11. *f* repeats the subject, Horus. ***34**, 1ff.: epithets of Horus. 1: § 113b. 2: § 89. 3: § 81. 6: § 113b. 8: § 118. 11: *nḏm.w* § 80. ***35**, 2: § 124b. 5: *mrw.t.f* "love to him". 6: "father": Osiris. 9: the office of the god-king. ***36**, 1: "it" is omitted § 133. 2: § 87. ***36**, 3—11: appeal to the visitors of the grave. 3: § 70; *nty.w* § 141. 4: § 105. 5: § 116. 6: § 135. 7: § 126. ***37**, 1—11: victory of Thutmose III. over Naharina (Mesopotamia). 1: § 64b: *pfꜣ* § 57c. 3: *r* "more than". 4: § 106. 5—7: § 127. 7: *nn* § 57. 9: § 125b. ***38**, 1—**39**, 4: a god-king speaks to Thutmose III.; the suffix "I", "my" is usually not written. 4: § 102. 11 *tꜣw* and 39, 1 *ẖ.wt*: written as plural in accordance with § 36a. ***39**, 1: *(y)ẖm.w* "those who know (thee) not" with the antique inital *y*. 2: *rn.y* § 58. 4: § 128.
39**, 5—11: Senmut (4**, 9), favourite of queen Hatshepsut (represented as king), is proud of his exalted position. 10: § 111.
***40**, 1—**41**, 6: Amenemheb relates his warlike deeds under Thutmose III.; the suffix of the first person singular is often not written. ***40**, 2: "he wished that"; *yry* § 63. 4: *ẖft*: conjunction "when" with the tense *śḏm.f*. 8: *ym.śn*: among the barbarians.
***40—41**, 1: § 41. 3: § 59. ***41**, 7—**42**, 4: monument which Thutmose III. presented to the high-priest *Nb-wꜥ.wy* as a proof of favour. 7: *dy.w* "given", namely the stone. ***42**, 2: § 55, 54.
***42**, 5—**43**, 2: Sinuhe relates his fight with a Syrian hero. 6: a hero without his like. 7: "he said that". ***43**, 2: war-god Mont *(mntw)*. ***43**, 3—**44**, 8: Sinuhe relates bis flight as deserter from the left bank of the Nile to Syria by way of the Egyptian fortresses at the Bitter Lakes. 4: § 141c. 5: § 111; *ẖd* from the way northward to land. 6: § 94, 133. 7: § 63. 8: § 128. 11: *n* "on account of". ***44**, 3: § 55. 4: § 41. 8: § 120. ***44**, 9—**45**, 11: a man relates his ship-wreck in the Red Sea. ***44**, 9: *pry.w* § 82; *yw.n* § 134. 10: § 64. 11: *nty.w* § 141. ***45**, 1: § 138. 2: § 82. 5; § 132a. 7: § 120. ***46**, 1—**48**, 11: a dragon-god appears to the ship-wrecked man and prophecies his deliverance. ***46**, 2: § 58. 3: § 132b. 11: § 134. ***47**, 2: § 137 *yn-m*. 5: § 82. 8: § 55. 9: § 58. ***48**, 2: from (the number of) the select. 7: § 103. 8: § 126a. 9: *rẖ.w.n.k* § 120. ***49**, 1—**50**, 11: song of

the harper, in the tomb of Neferhotep, who summons to enjoyment of life (in the vernacular § 8 c with article § 41). ***49,** 2: § 41. 5: *ḫpr* § 60. 8: *wtṯ*. 11: § 100. ***50,** 1: § 101a. 4: *ś.nḏm.t* § 33g. 7: § 136; *pfꜣ* § 57c. 8: *mry* § 113a. 11: § 55. ***51,** 1—**53,** 11: battle of Rameses II. against the Kheta (Hittites) on the Orontes. Report in the vernacular. ***51,** 1: § 64. 3: § 80. 4: § 138; *r-ḏd* "thats" 5: § 133. 7: § 141. 9: § 64b, § 128b. ***53,** 3: § 132b. 4: § 87. 8: 133. **50,** 4: "hour" of rage. ***54,** 1—11: Una elateiy his warlike deeds (ancient language; suffix first singular is usualla not written). 4: *r* "more than". 5: § 81. 6: § 95; first the matre" lis given, then the object. 7: § 130. 8: *ḫr-hꜣ.t* antique for *m-ḥꜣ. t* at the head of" § 62a. 10: *ḫry.w.šC*. 11: § 54, 66b.
***55,** 1—11: hymn of Amenophis IV. to the sun-god Aton. 1: § 66a. 2: § 70. 5: § 134. 7: § 124a. 8: conjecture "it" after *ś.Cnḫ* § 133. 9: the names of the countries are removed from the sentence and are repiesented by *s(ꜣ) nb*. 11: *ḫry* § 63; *wnm* "(corn-)food".
***56,** 1—7: a sage gives the king advice how to enjoy himself. 1: § 102, 18c. 3: § 126b. 4: § 105, 110. ***56,** 8—11: prologue and epilogue of a chapter of the Book of the Dead. 8: § 139. 9: § 135, 68. 10: § 96. 11: § 118.

Index.

(Index in completion of the table of contents.)

Lesestücke

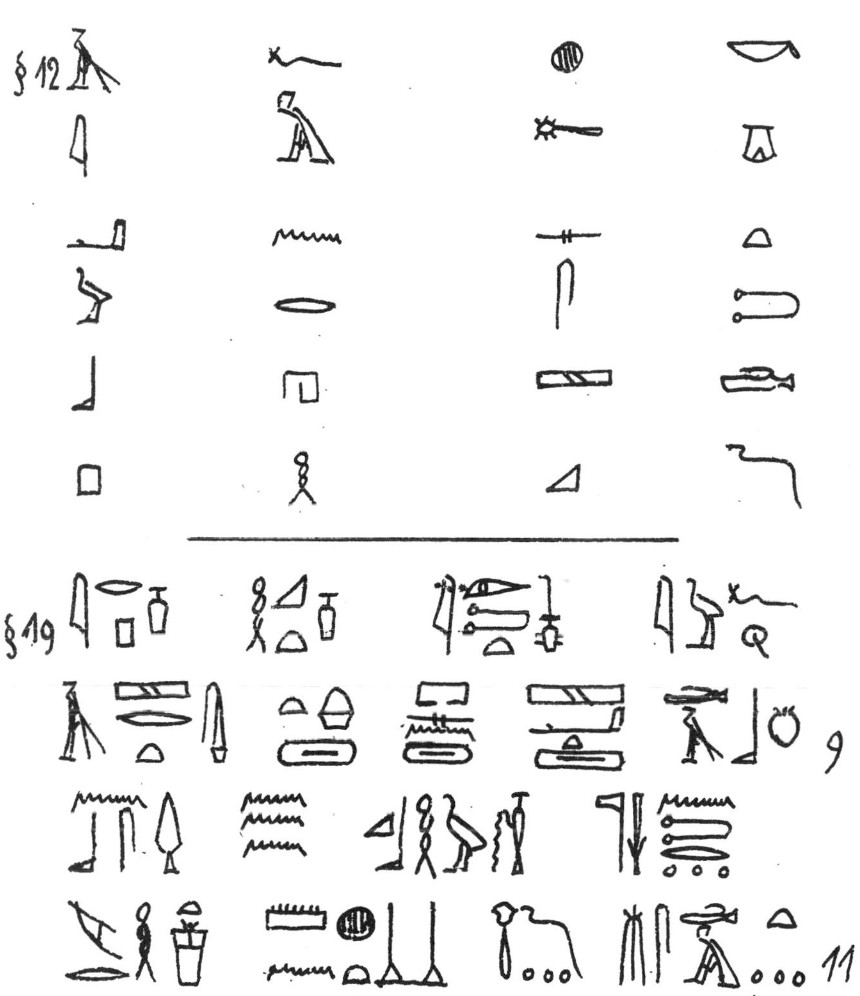

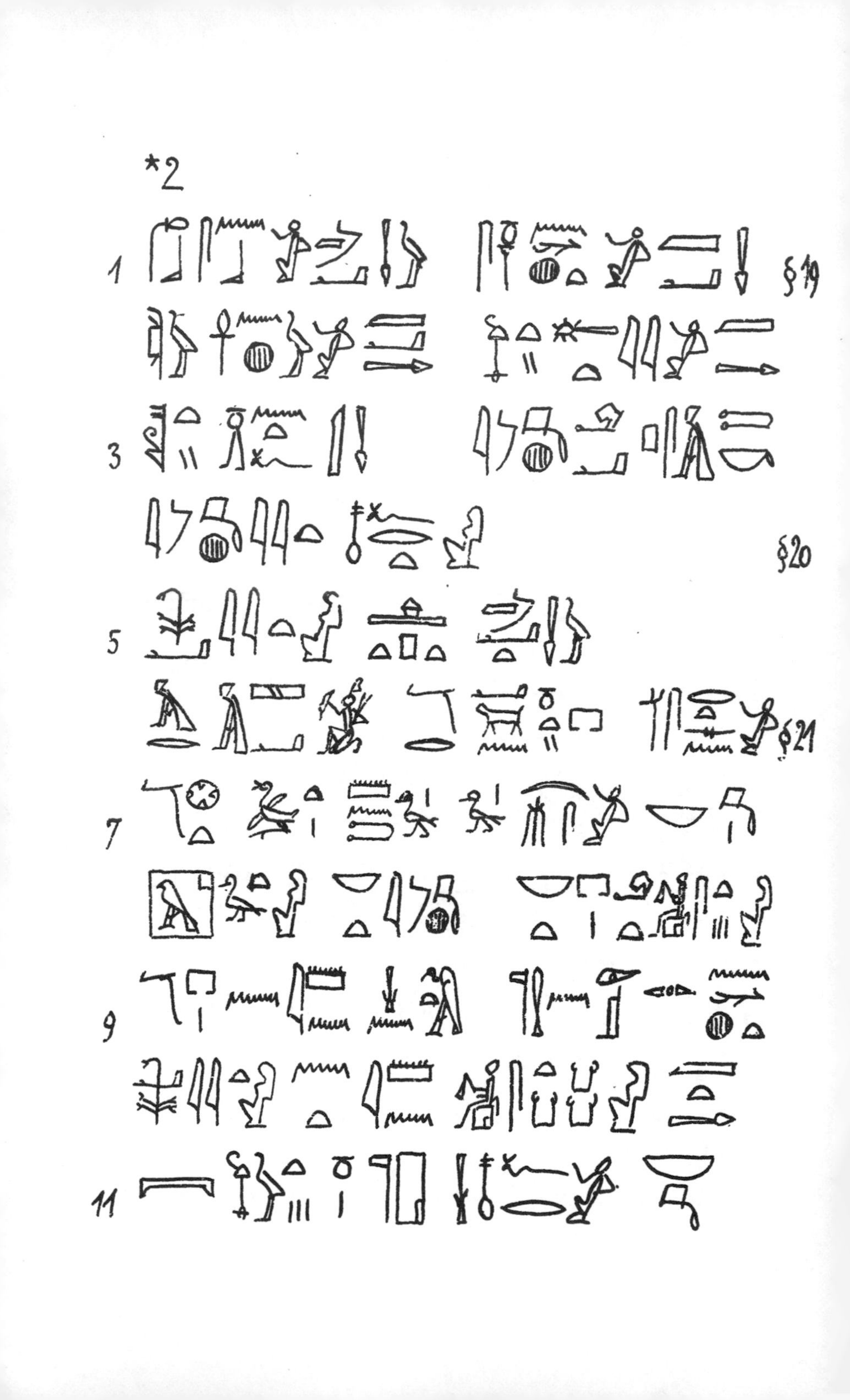

*2

1 §19

3

§20

5

§21

7

9

11

*3

§22 1

3

§26 5

7

9

11

*4

1 §40

3

§43

5

7

9

11

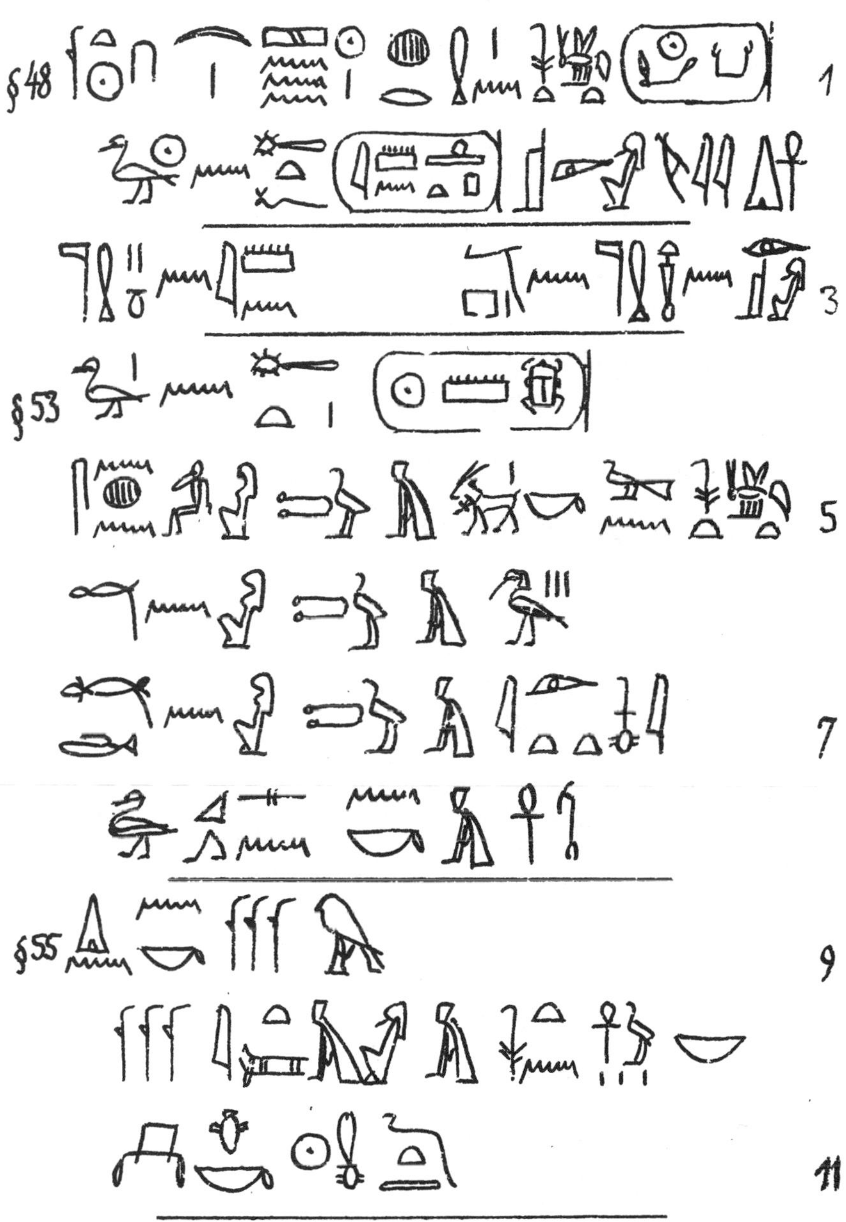
*5
§48
§53
§55

*6

§61

§61

§63

*8

§63

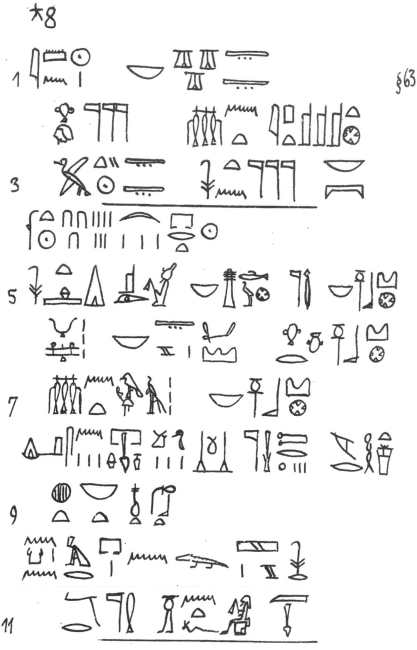

*10

1

3 §64

5

7

9 §106

11

*11

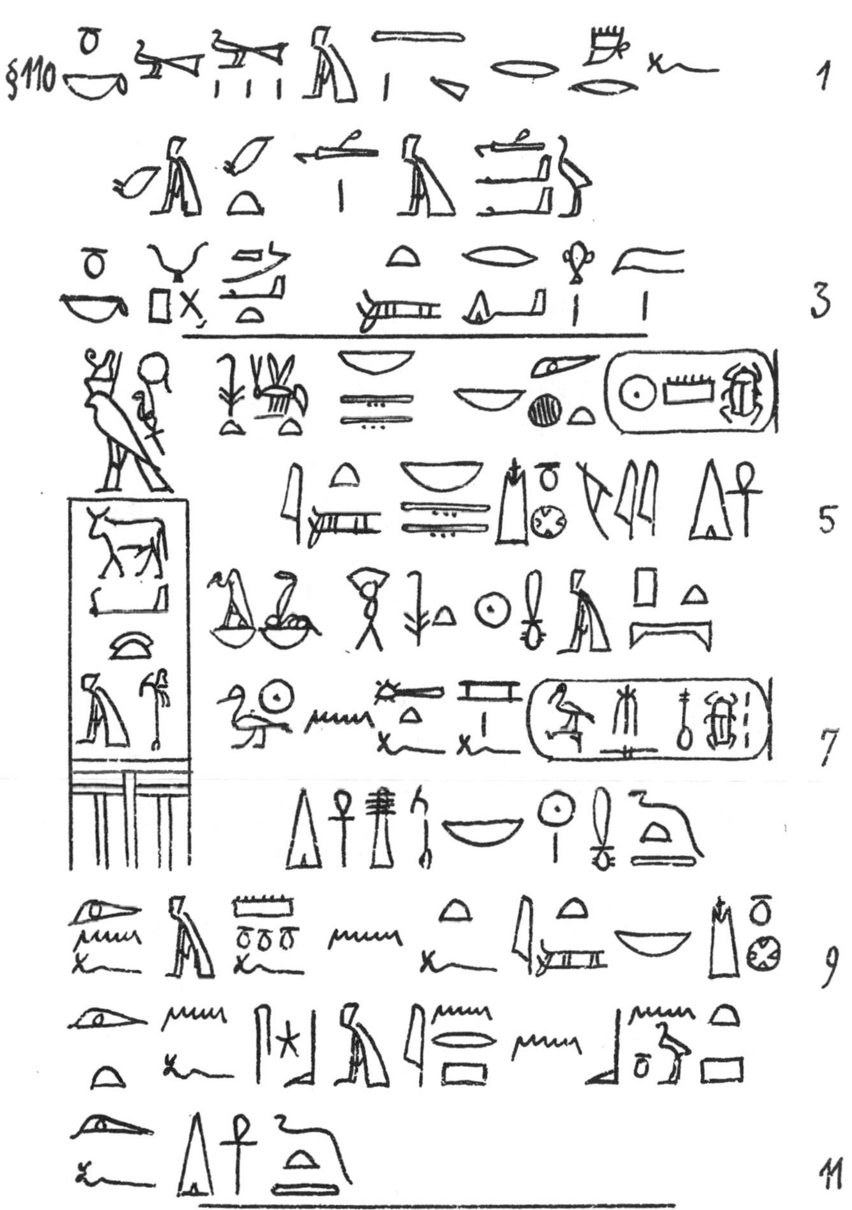

*12

§111

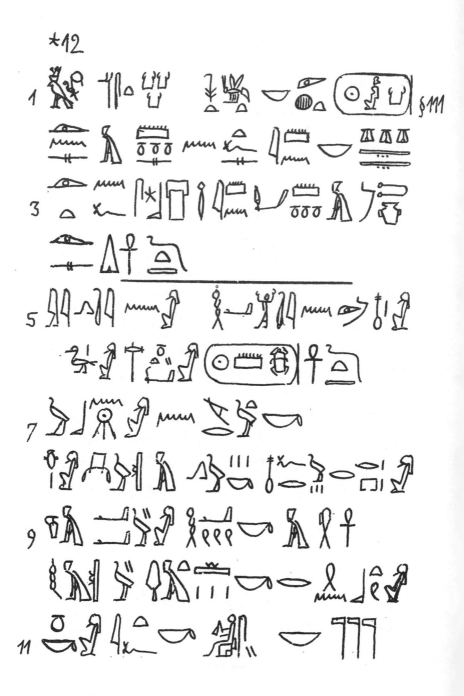

*13

§111

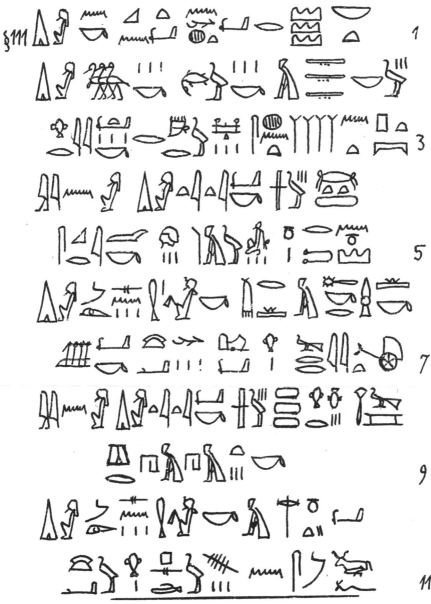

*14

1 §115

3

5

7

9

11

* 15

§ 116 1

3

5

7

9

11

*16

§ 117

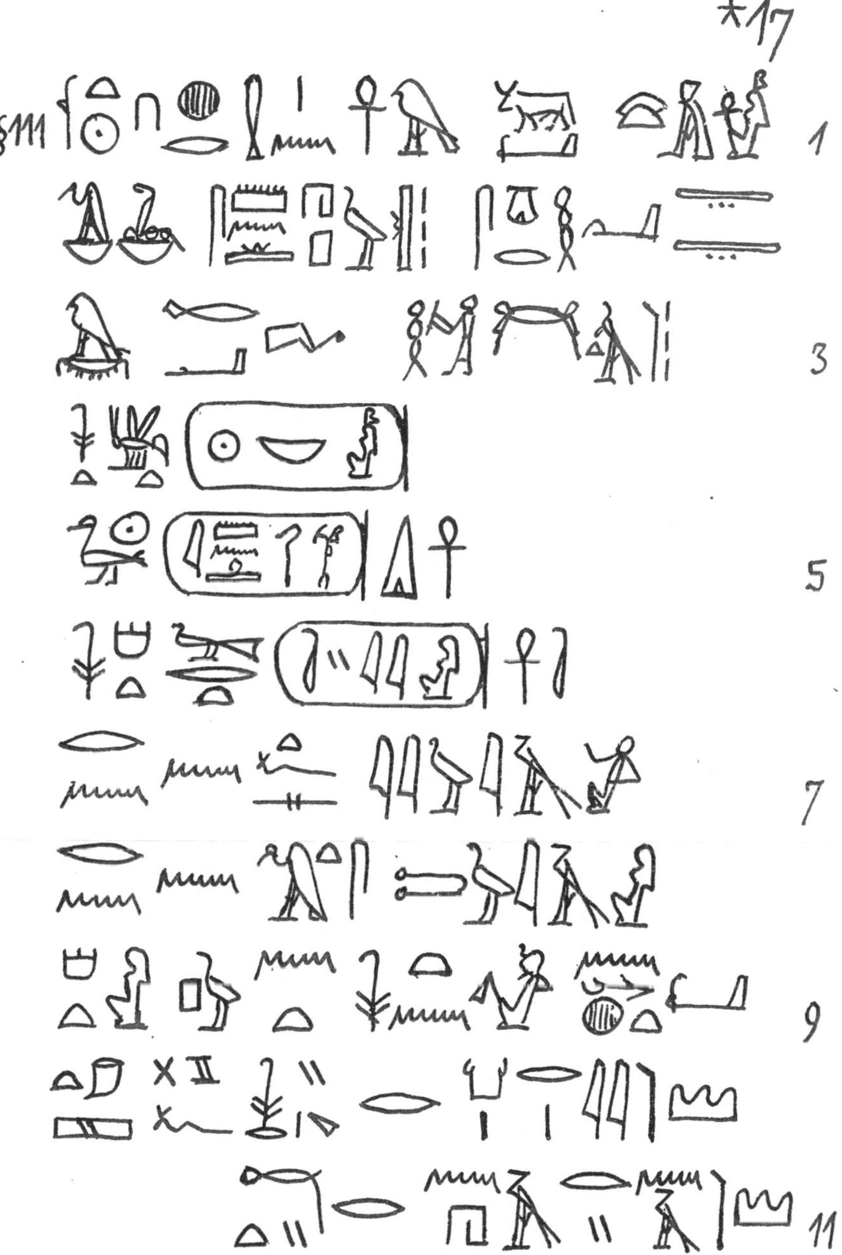
*17
§111

*18

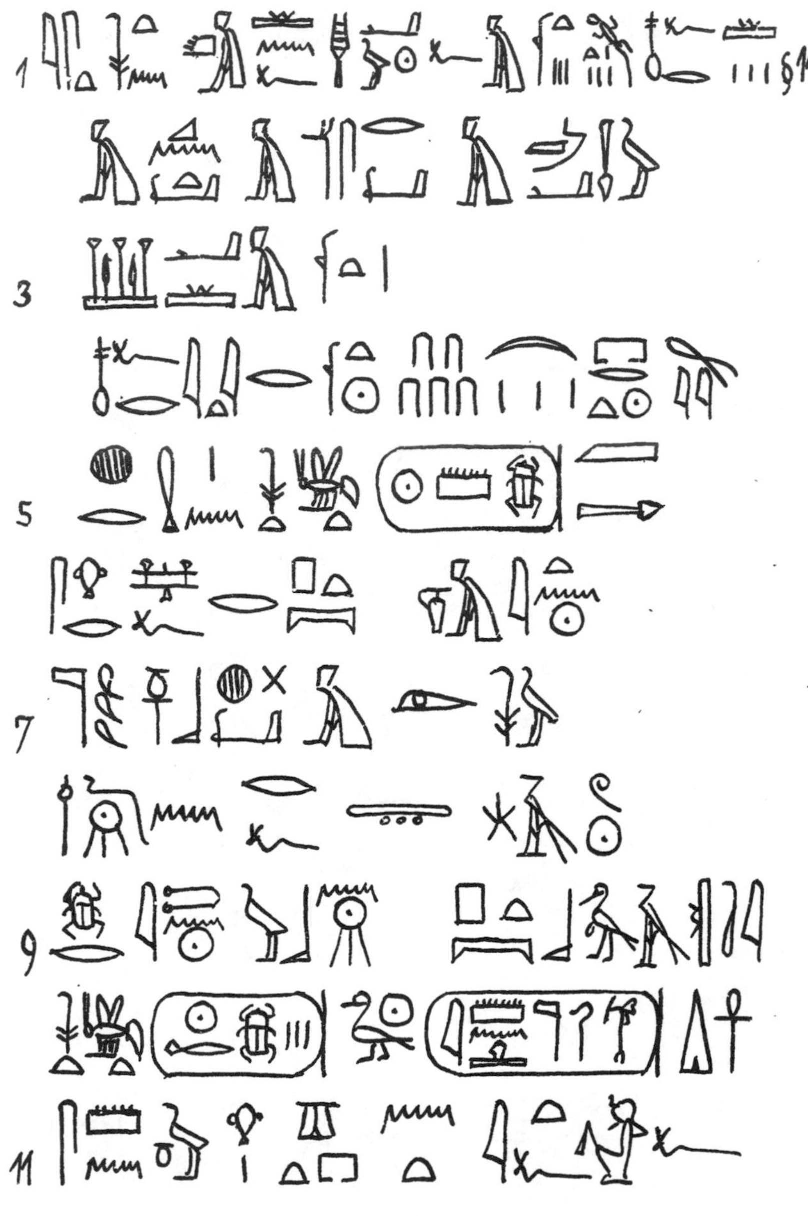

*19

§111

§120

*20

§120

*21

§120

*22

§120

*23

120

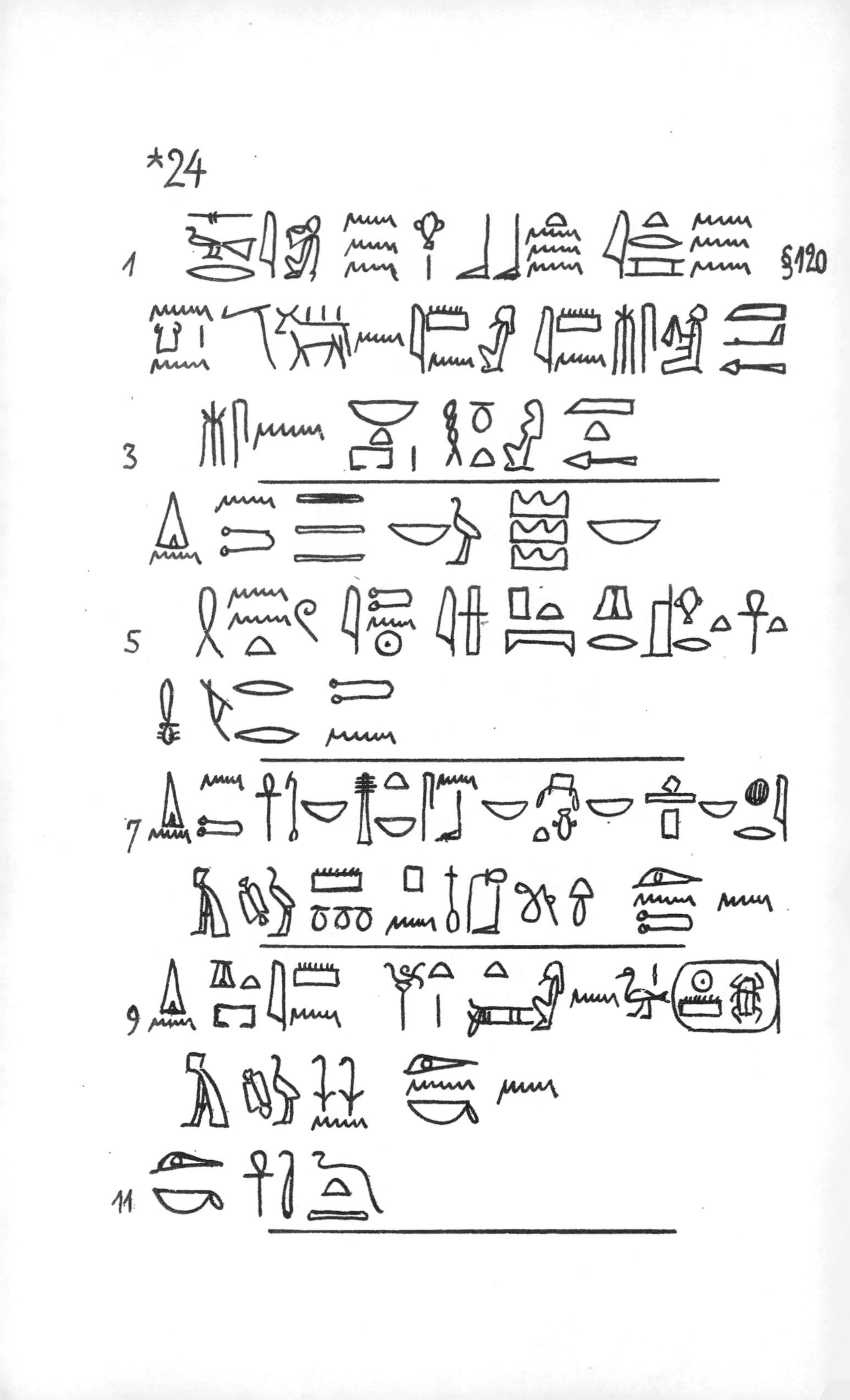

*24

§120

§120

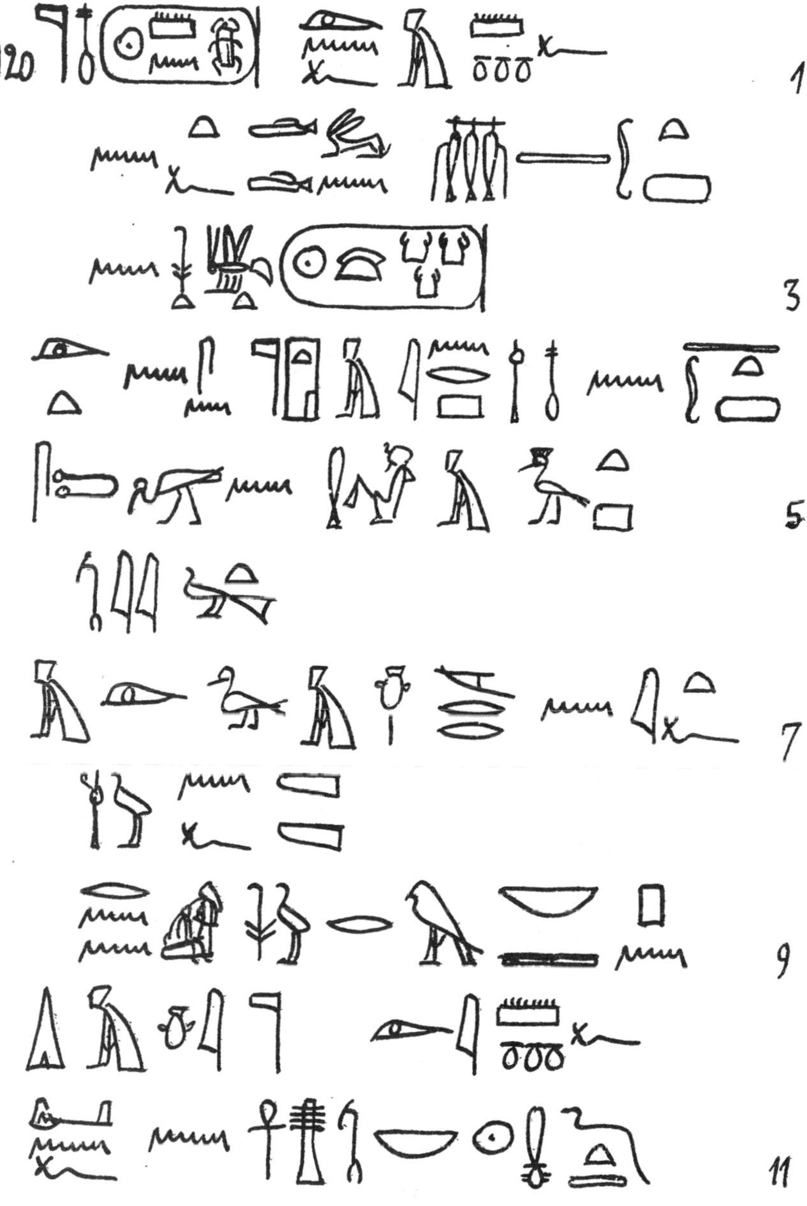

*26

§120

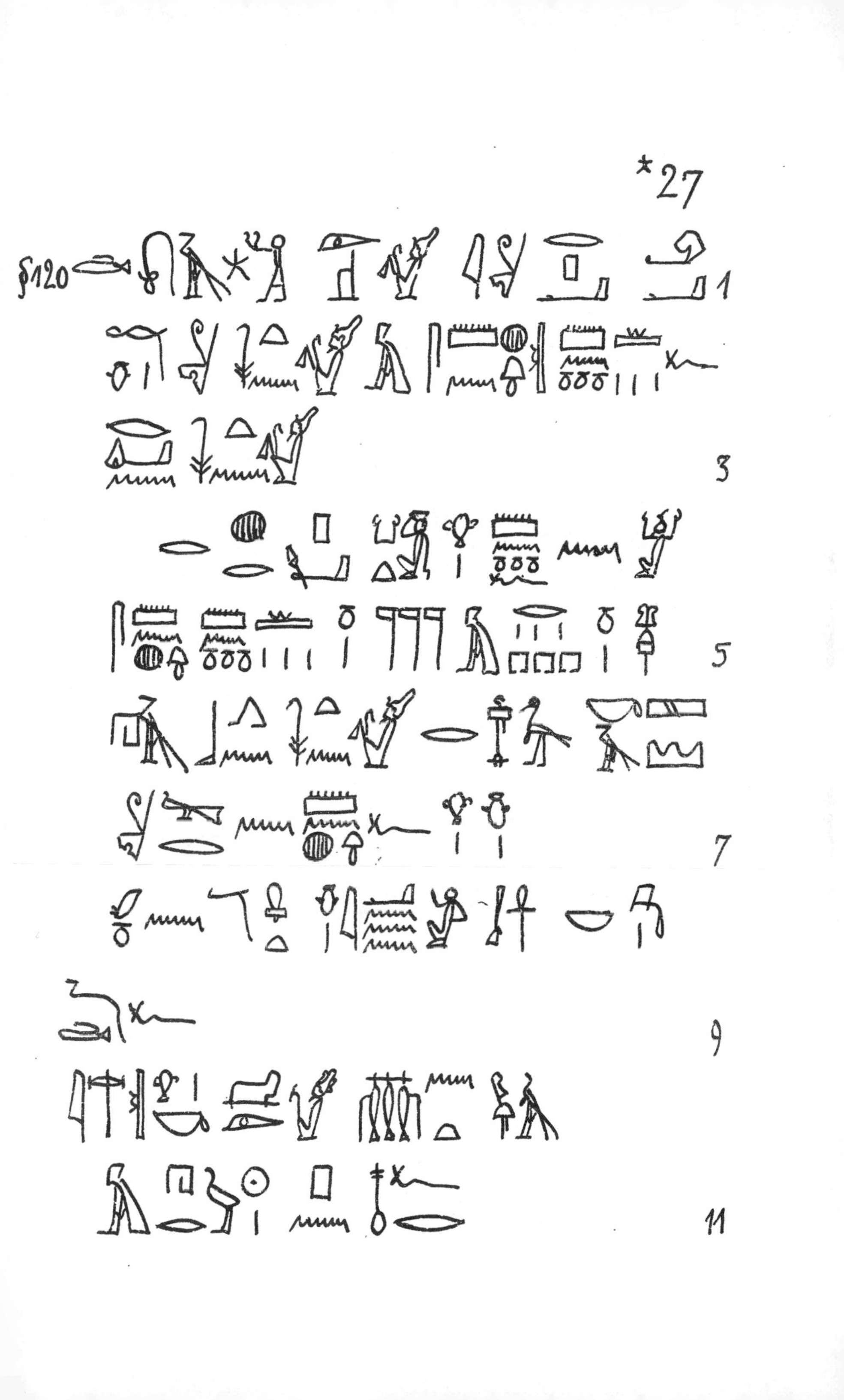

*27

§120

*28

§120

*29

§120

§122

*30

§122

§125

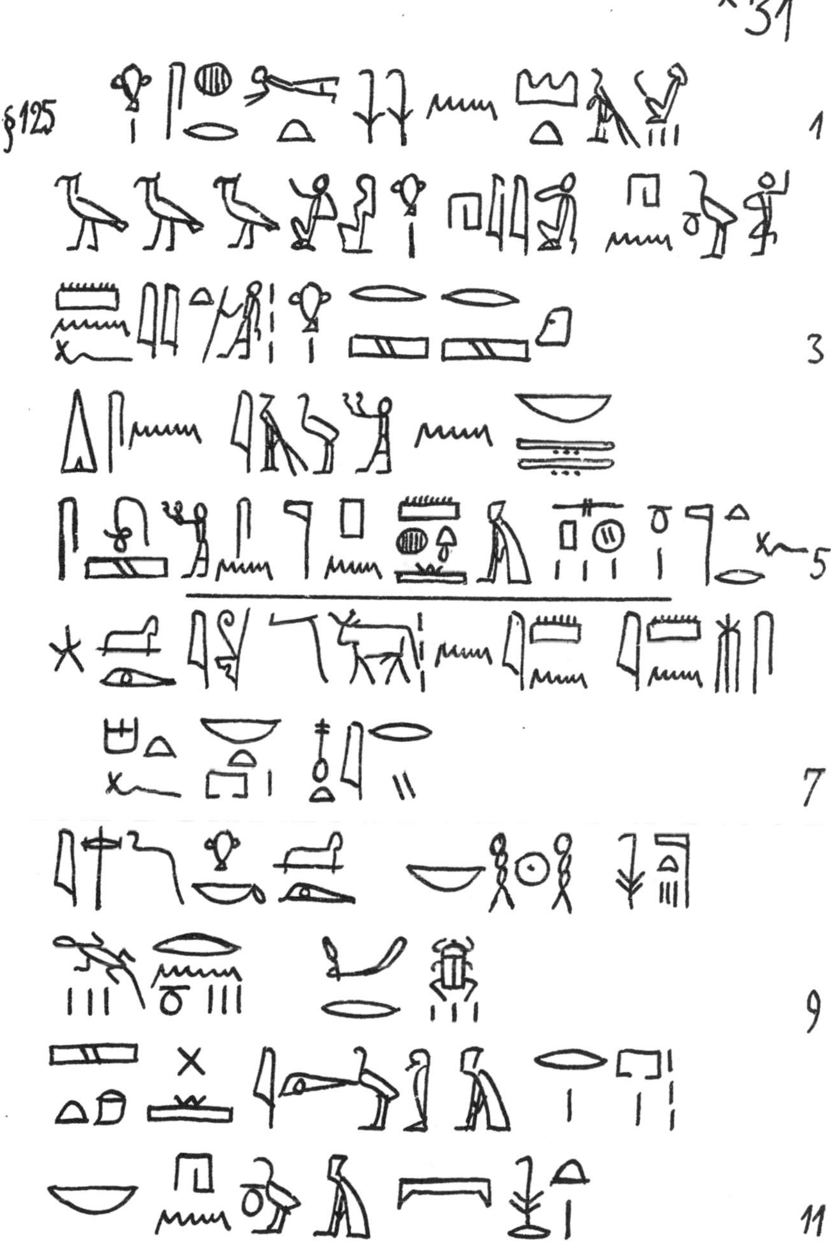

*32

§125

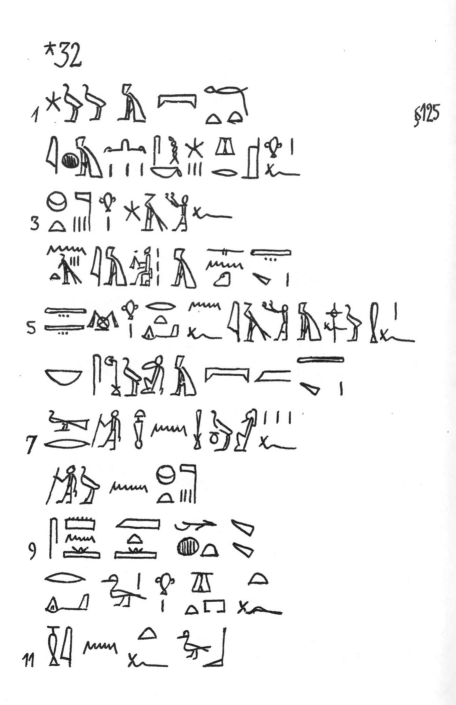

*33

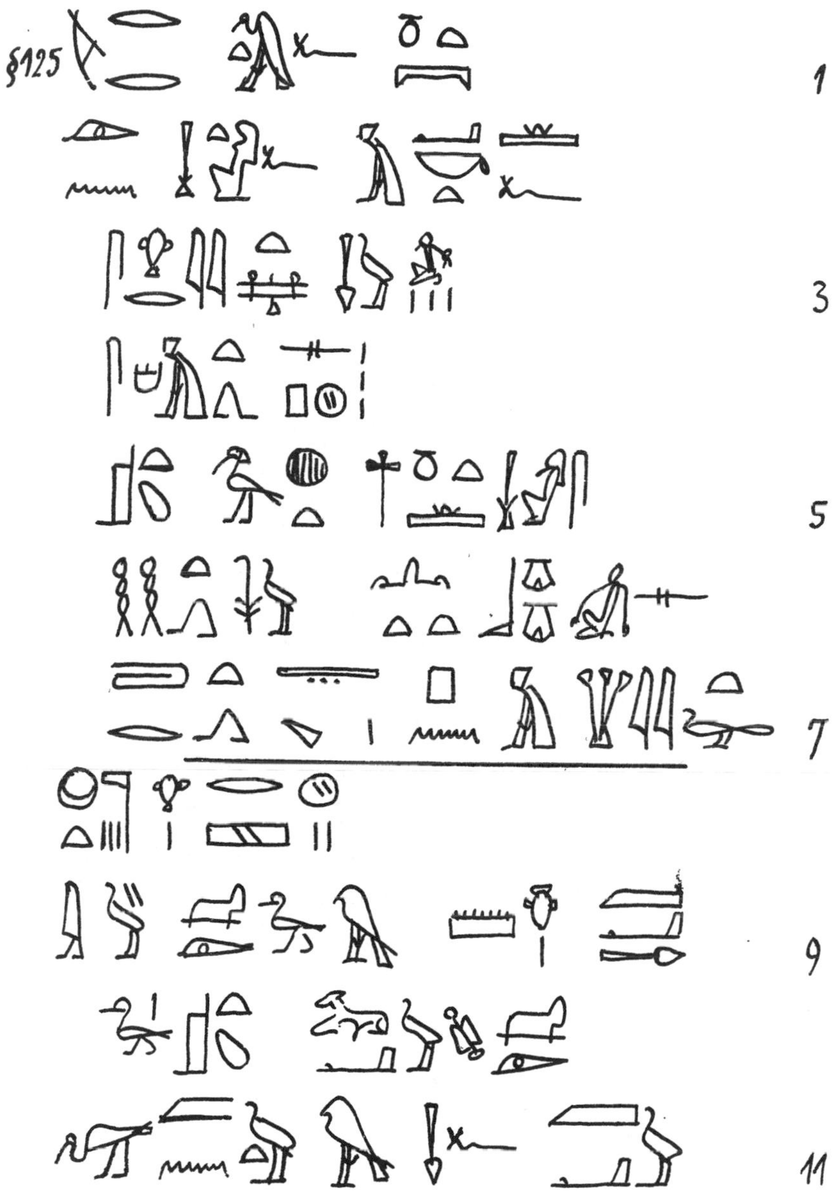

*34

§125

§125

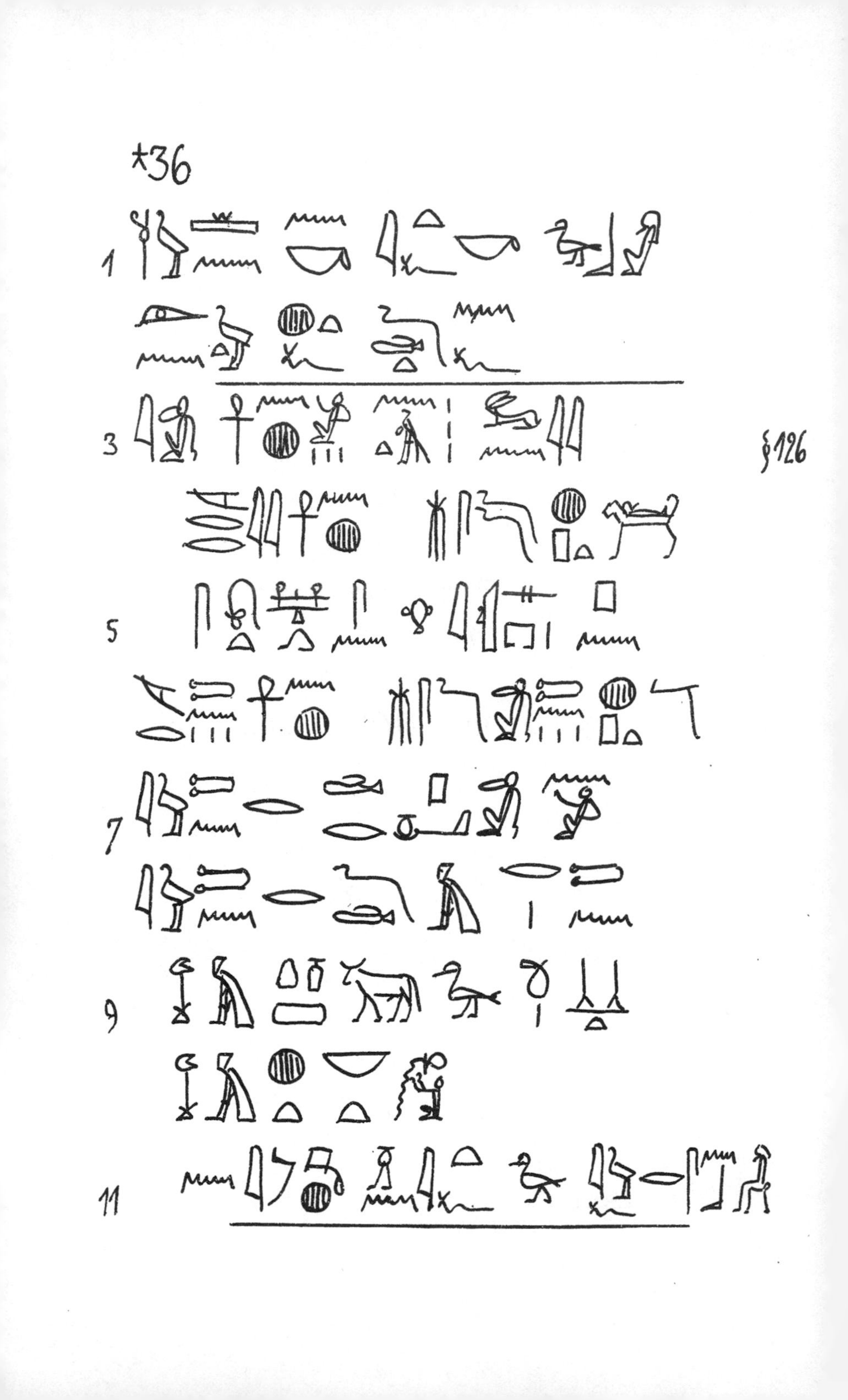

*36

1

3 §126

5

7

9

11

§127

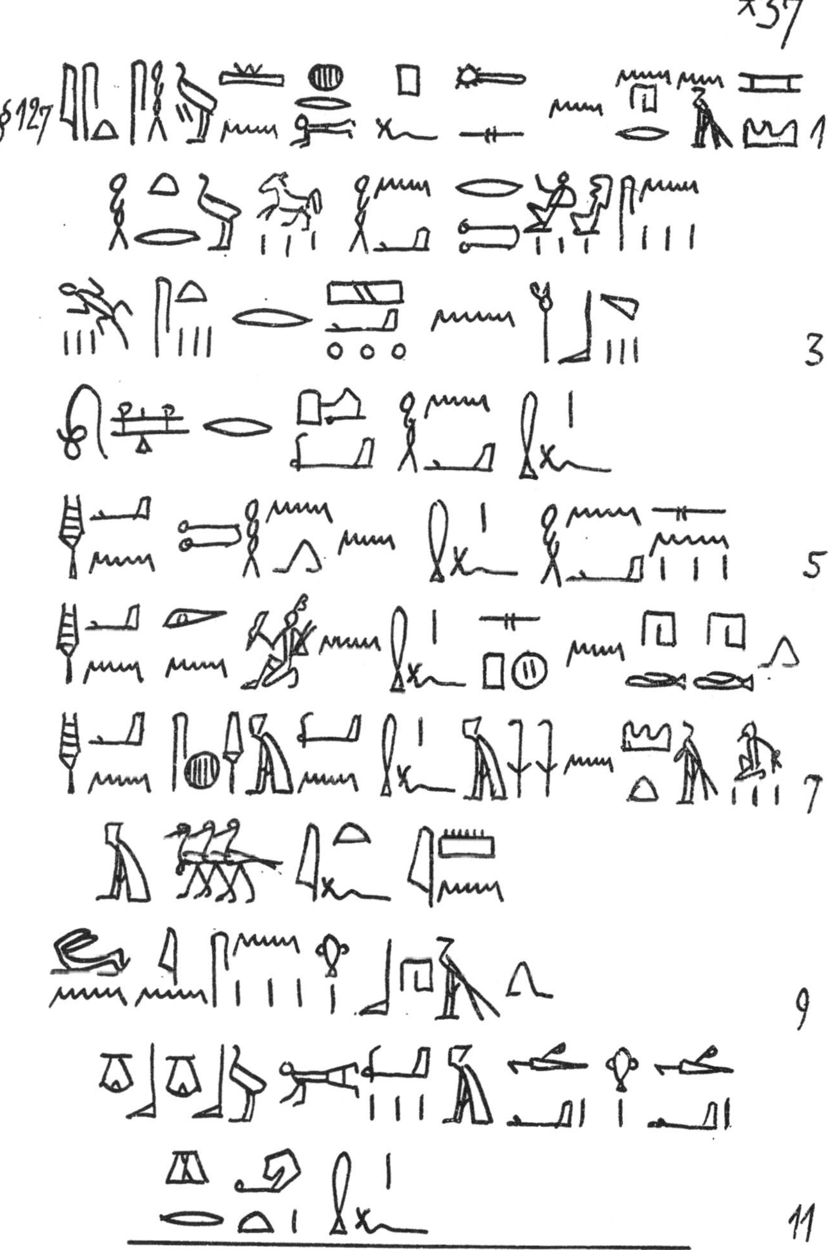

*38

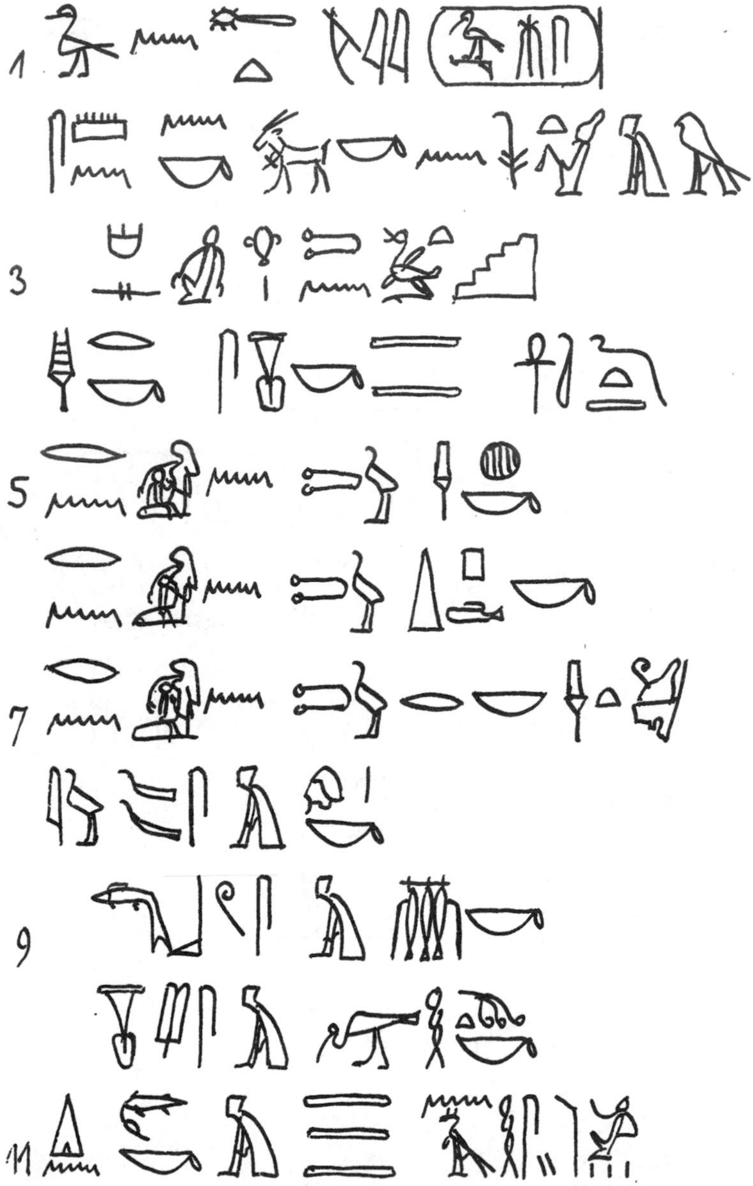

§ 133

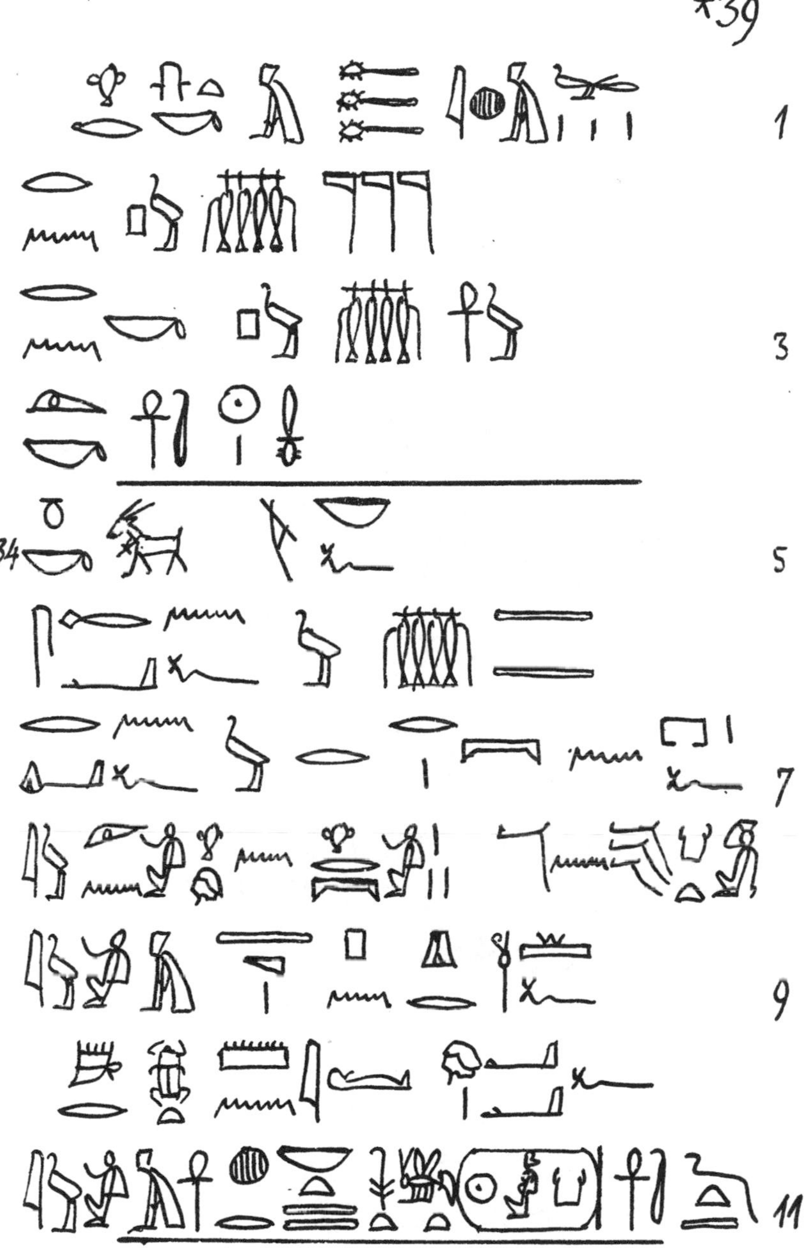
*39
§134

*40

1 § 136

3

5

7

9

11

§136

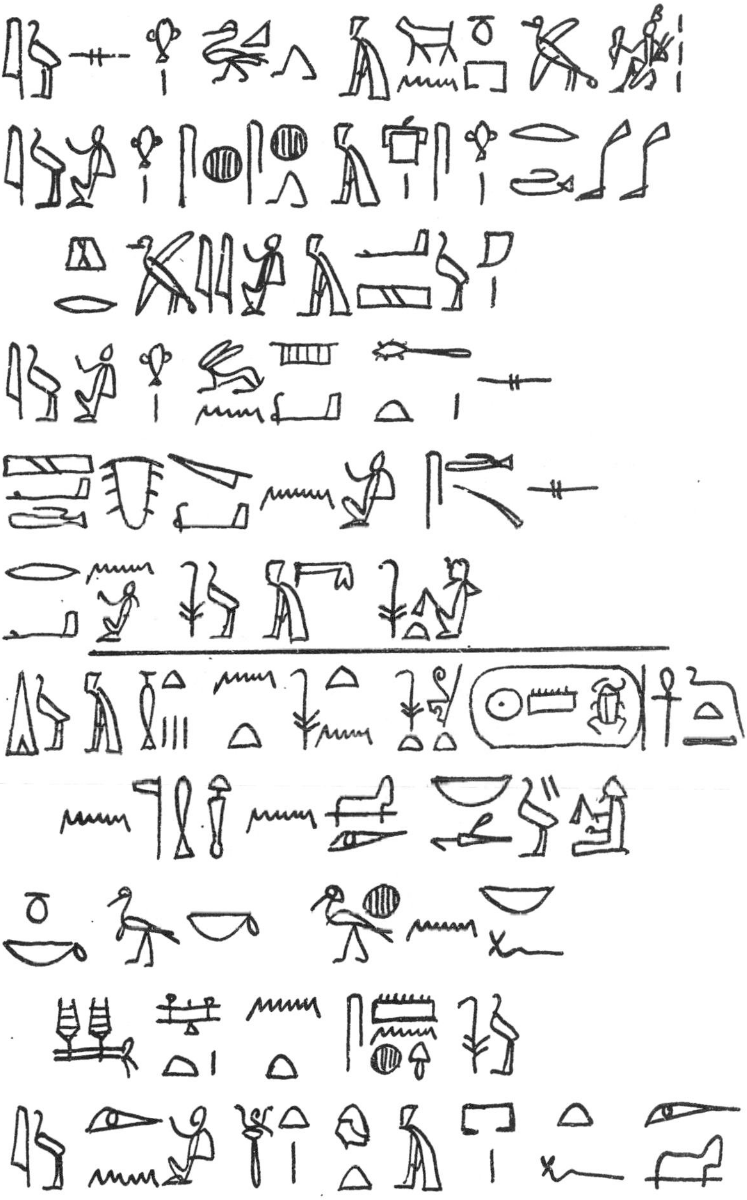

*42

§139

*43

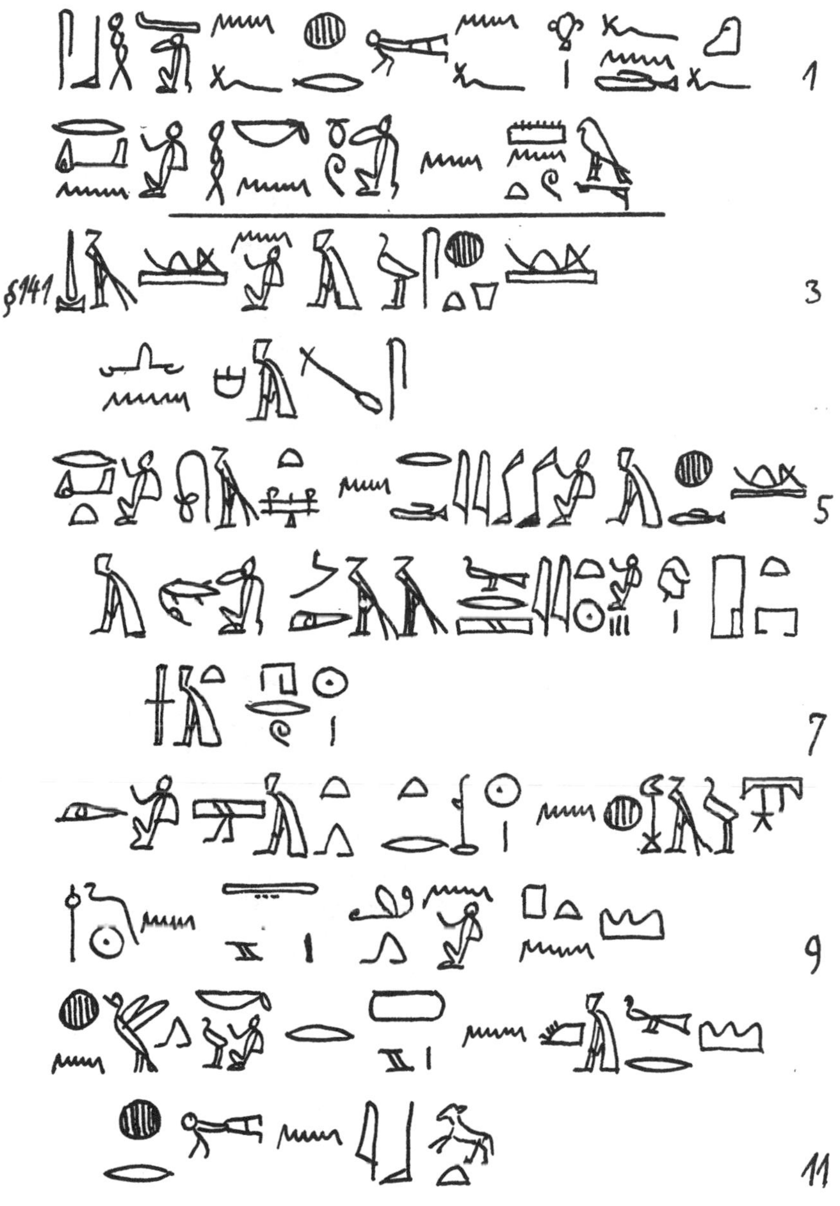

*44

§141

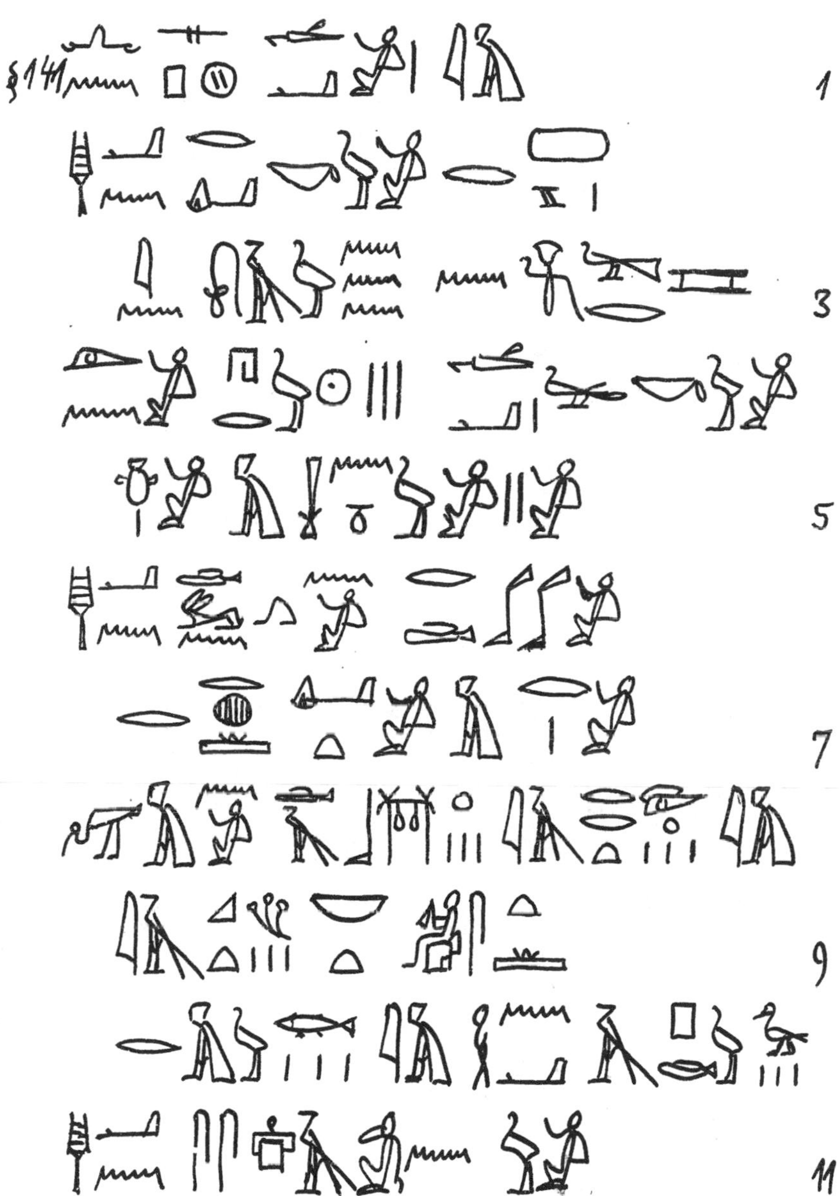
§141

*46

§141

*47

§141

*48

§141

*49

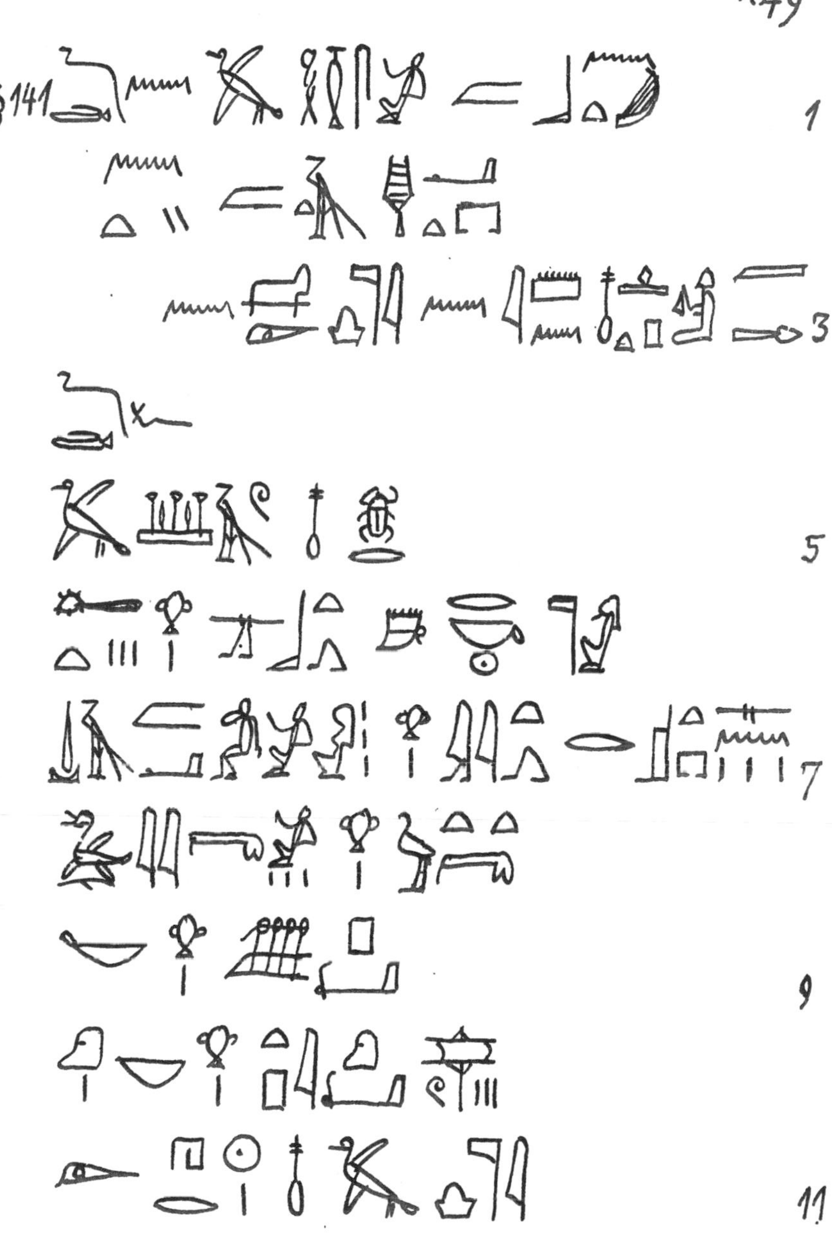

*50

§141

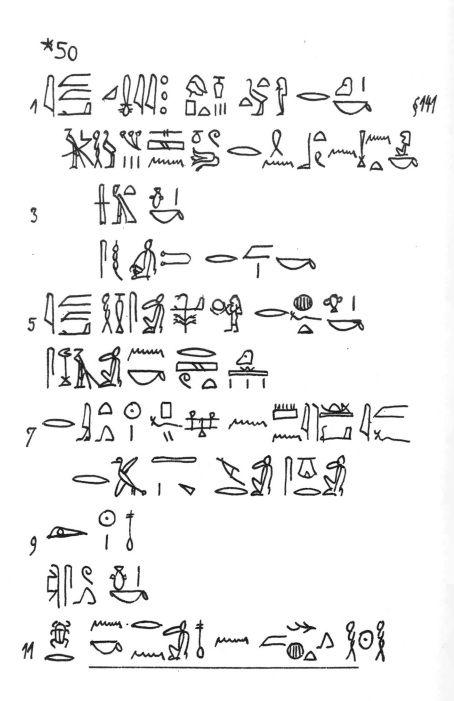

§ 141

*52

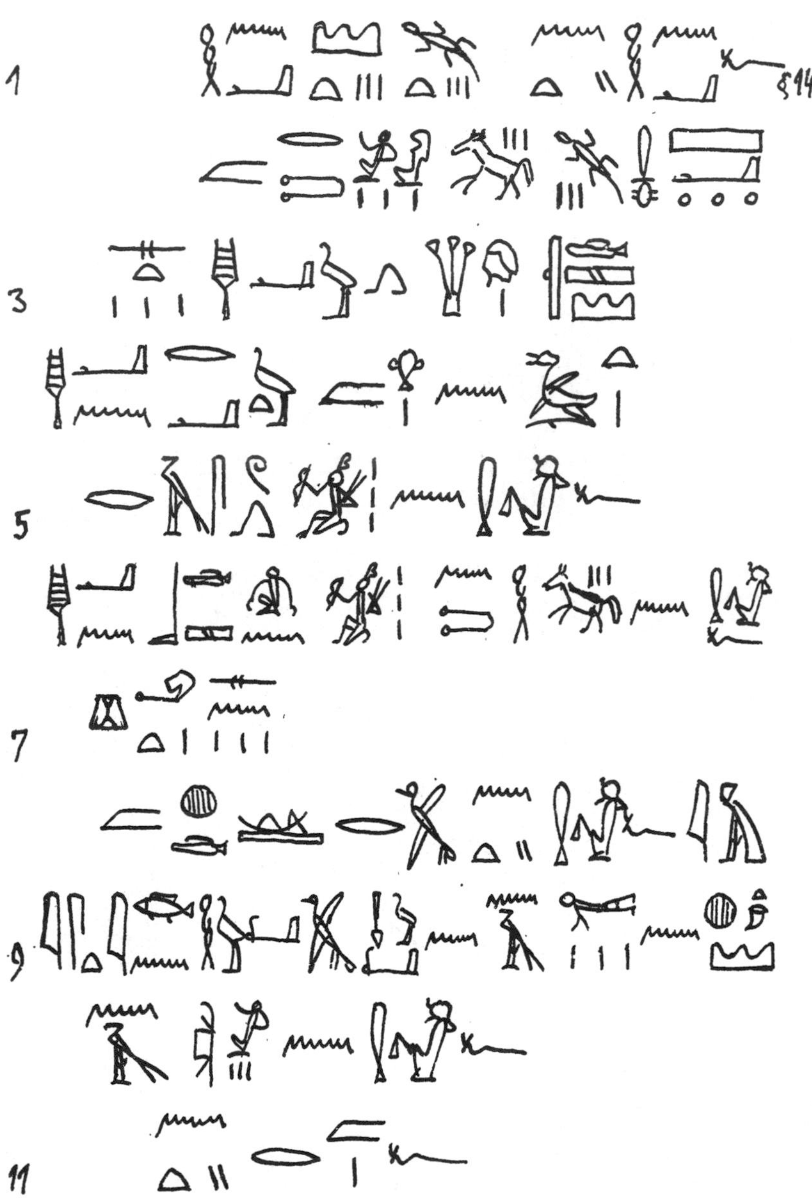

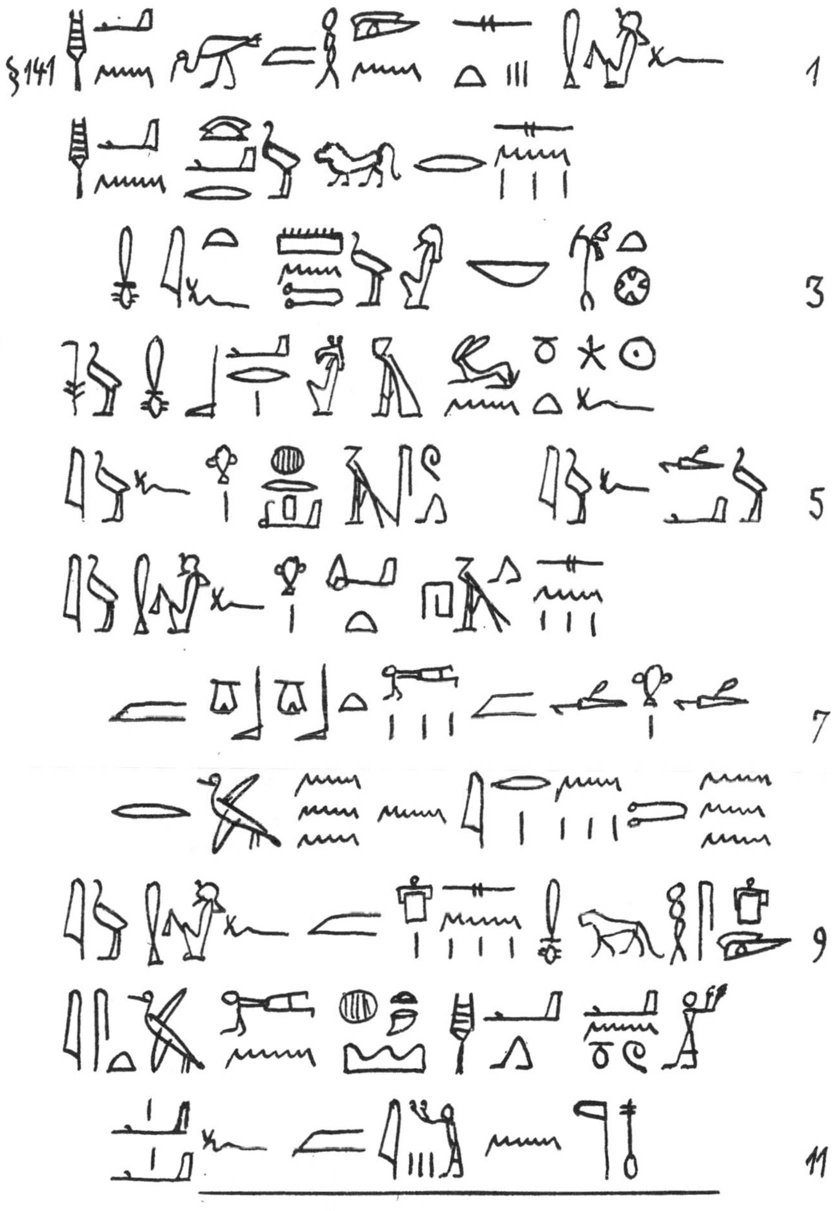

*54

§141

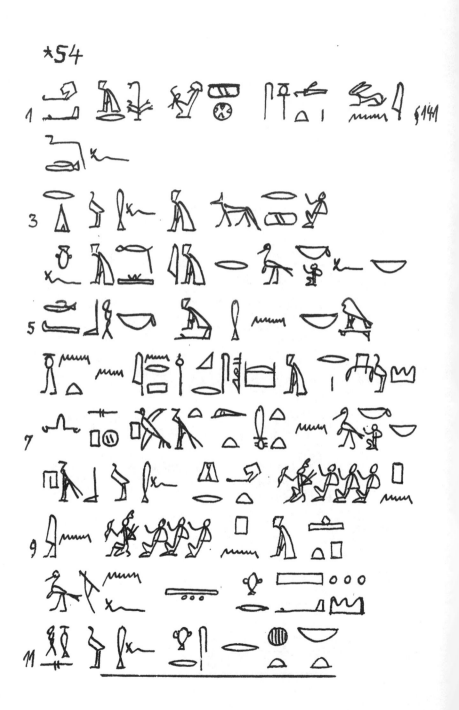

*55

§141

*56

§141